PRACTIC
FENG SHUI
FOR THE HOME

PRACTICAL
FENG SHUI
FOR THE HOME

Albert Low

Pelanduk
Publications

This book is for my parents and Ancestors,
whose roots cherished forth
a Pathfinder.

Published by
Pelanduk Publications (M) Sdn. Bhd.,
24 Jalan 20/16A, 46300 Petaling Jaya,
Selangor Darul Ehsan, Malaysia.

Address all correspondence to
Pelanduk Publications (M) Sdn. Bhd.,
P.O. Box 8265, 46785 Kelana Jaya,
Selangor Darul Ehsan, Malaysia.

1st printing March 1995
2nd printing November 1995

Perpustakaan Negara Malaysia   Cataloguing-in-Publication Data

Low, Albert
    Practical Feng Shui for the home / Albert Low.
    ISBN 967-978-523-8
    1. Feng-shui. 2. Geomancy. I. Title.
    133.333

Printed in Malaysia by
Academe Art & Printing Services Sdn. Bhd.

Contents

Contents

the knobs … 191\Toilet fronting … 192\Fortune flowing out … 193\Townhouse: Where to put the door … 194\Seeing eye-to-eye

Preface

THE DEBUT OF the "Ancient Chinese Art of Feng Shui" as a regular column in *The Star* had generated much interest and a great following among the readers. To date thousands of letters have been received, and queries continue to pour in every week. However, due to the overwhelming response, sadly to say, not all of them could be attended to.

Practical Feng Shui for the Home is a collection of specially selected articles that were published in the above-mentioned daily. It is unique and unlike other feng shui books because it is a Yang book: it responses to the seekers or enquirers with solutions to their queries. Practical suggestions are always given so that they can live in harmony with their environment.

It is presented in twenty-five parts, each delving into a major topic pertinent to the home—bedrooms, kitchen, gates, windows, etc. In the process of doing so, the author also provides insights into how a feng shui master analyses the various situations encountered in his work, charting his approach in furnishing the enquirers with the best solutions to their problems.

THE PUBLISHER

Acknowledgement

THE PUBLICATION OF this book has been possible largely because of the readers' enthusiasm and support for my column in *The Star*. In return, the paper's support team has played their roles magnificently in responding to the readers' interest.

A hearty thank you is due to the Managing Director of *The Star*, Steven Tan, Group Chief Editor, Ng Poh Tip, "Section 2" Editor, Gilbert Yap, Chief Sub-Editor, Oh Cheng Bee, Senior Writer, Lim Cheng Hoe, and all those who had lent a helping hand in making the Feng Shui column a success.

I also like to thank the publisher and the staff of Pelanduk Publications for their hard work in bringing this work into fruition.

The Author

SINCE HIS SCHOOL-DAYS, the author has been fascinated by the supernatural and the unknown. This yen for understanding led him to join a religious order. After four years of disciplined training, he left to seek his own truth. His search brought him before palmists, yogis, monks, Taoist masters, and even cave hermits, who shared their wisdom with him. As his interest was in the world psychic phenomena, he began to excel in this area.

Upon leaving school, he joined the insurance industry, where he built his career for seven years, consequently becoming the top agent in his company.

His first writing stint was for the Palmistry column in *Her World* magazine, in 1980–1981. His earliest feng shui article appeared in 1988 in the *New Straits Times*. Spurred by the positive response of that article, he began writing more frequently on the subject. In 1990 he began his weekly feng shui column in *The Star*.

Based in Kuala Lumpur, Albert Low is an associate member of the Society for Psychical Research, UK. He now has behind him over 25 years of study on feng shui and psychic phenomena.

His first book, *Feng Shui: The Way to Harmony*, published by Pelanduk Publications in 1993, is now in its third print. It has recently been translated into Bahasa Indonesia for the Indonesian market. *Practical Feng Shui for the Home* is his second book.

PART 1

General Queries

Give exact details of home and surroundings

DO THE FOLLOWING objects play a part in feng shui?
- ☐ *Lamp-post at the left-hand corner of the house.*
- ☐ *Telephone-post at the right-hand corner, at the back of the house.*
- ☐ *Hump lying across the road.*

Mrs KGL
Petaling Jaya

THE ABOVE IS the exact wording of your letter and it is rather vague. For instance, is the telephone-post at the right-hand corner of the house, or is it really in the left-hand corner (which is on your right if you are facing it)?

Without an exact picture or description of your house and the surrounding objects, it would be difficult to assess the situation properly or safely.

To get some free feng shui tips here and there, readers should in turn provide precise details of their home and surroundings. A drawing, a picture or even photographs would be very useful to the geomancer in studying your situation before coming to a conclusion.

Sometimes, an inexperienced observer may not be able to accurately convey his findings, thereby confusing the person who receives the information.

Remember that you act as the eyes of the geomancer in this case. If you view something wrongly, you will describe it wrongly. Even if you view something correctly but describe it wrongly, the result is the same. So please bear this in mind when sending in requests for help.

Books

I AM INTERESTED in learning more about feng shui. Can you recommend books on the subject and places where I can buy them? Also, let me know what the cost of the books would be like.

Lee Bah Ong
Penang

FOR A START, the books on feng shui listed below will be of help. These books can easily be found in major bookstores. If you cannot find them, perhaps you could ask the manager to order a copy for you.

I cannot give you the prices of these books as these may vary from time to time and at different bookshops.

Remember that knowledge is power, and it is so much more precious when used to your benefit. It cannot be stolen. The owner of knowledge should be proud that he has enriched his soul with it.

True knowledge endures without regard for the passage of time or the immutable laws of the universe. Anyway, here is the list:

Feng Shui: The Way of Harmony by Albert Low (Pelanduk Publications); *Chinese Geomancy* by Evelyn Lip; *Feng Shui for the Home* by the same author; *Feng Shui* by Sarah Rossbach; *Interior Design with Feng Shui* by Derek Walters; *The Living Earth Manual of Feng Shui* by Steven Skinner; *Feng Shui* by Ernest Eitel; and *The Book of Chinese Beliefs* by Frena Bloomfield.

Afraid renovations will bring bad luck

TWO YEARS AGO, a feng shui expert from Hong Kong visited my house. I told him how I missed the Empat Ekor prizes on many occasions. He moved around the hall with his feng shui instrument and concluded that I should enter the house from the left side of the front of the house, or by the back door.

Then a year ago, I had some extensions done, and fixed a sliding door for the front of the house. Now I have second thoughts on whether I should follow the feng shui master's advice and open a new door on the left side, to bring me luck. But I also fear that such a move may adversely affect my children who hold good jobs and are doing well.

Please advise.

Curious
Petaling Jaya

WITHOUT ANY DESCRIPTION or a sketch of your house, it is hard to offer any suggestions.

Since you plan to do some renovations, and fear any adverse implications, why not engage a professional geomancer to help you out? This will be money well spent. It's better than finding out too late that your renovations were wrongly done and need to be rectified.

Advice from friends

THERE IS A TREE opposite my house which faces directly my main gate and door. Upon the advice of my friends, I did some renovation to ward off the bad chi from the tree. I have extended my living room and relocated my front door to the side. It has been some months now, but things have not changed for the better.

What do you advise?

Danny Chong
Penang

PERHAPS YOU SHOULD consider a couple of other points too. Is there any sharp angle from a neighbouring house which faces the new door? If so, then it is very bad feng shui for your house.

Besides, have you been properly advised by your friends? It is always good to seek professional advice to ensure that the renovations

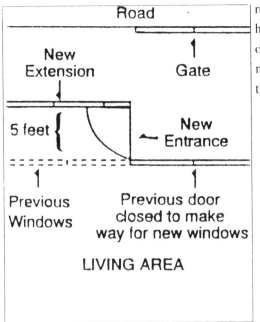

recommended are in harmony with the rest of the house, or you might end up worse off than before.

Is ignorance bliss?

I AM AN avid reader of your column and I find it very interesting. However, I have also begun to find it rather depressing. In my opinion, there are many people in this world who become disillusioned and give a lot of negative 'feedback'. I am sure you do not want any part of them.

I am saying this because most of your articles talk about bad feng shui, like unfavourable fronting of homes, etc. In addition, you do not offer practical solutions to the problems.

As a house-owner, I can appreciate the upheaval and difficulties of moving house. Maybe giving lots of solutions would interfere with your business interests.

So as a suggestion, why not concentrate on the positive side like giving ideal locations/positions of homes and favourable fronting? In some ways, ignorance is bliss. You may not agree, but then again, we are each unique individuals in our own right. Hope to see more of your articles.

Chan
Penang

CONSTRUCTIVE CRITICISM IS always welcomed. After all, to err is human. Reading these articles, I hope, has not caused you to push the panic button at any time. If you find that you are overly sensitive in reading these articles, the best advice is to refrain from doing so.

Whether you are the type who is easily influenced or persuaded, or if you have a strong will and good judgement, is for you to find out. Your reaction would then depend on your character. The ancient Greek philosophy to "know thyself" still echoes strongly from the distant past.

For instance, if a person of weak character is easily frightened by tales of ghosts and weird happenings, then he should not talk of such things in the late, dark hours. If, then, he suffers from paranoid delusions and all sorts of phobias, he only has himself to blame.

You have to decide what is good for yourself, mentally, physically and spiritually. If you find that you are sensitive to certain knowledge or information, then do not entertain it in your mind but instead wipe off such disturbing thoughts.

In ancient times, men always lived close to nature. They built their homes to the contours of the terrain, to make sure that these buildings would be in harmony with their environment.

Time changes things. Nowadays, modern equipment and tools simple slice off or blow up certain 'intruding' portions of the landscape to make way for new buildings.

The eager buyers are satisfied, at the expense of nature. The objective is to maximize usage for maximum returns, but the penalty is always stiff.

When earlier issues of this column were written, I was not trying to cause trouble to home-owners. Why, in the first place, did I write such "negative" things? Well, if there is half a glass of water on the table, the man with the negative point of view will say it is half empty. And of course the one with the positive attitude sees it as half full.

"If you take the knowledge in a positive frame of mind . . . you have nothing to lose."

Once, an established shoe company in a developed country decided to send its salesmen to a remote country in Africa. Their job was to penetrate the untapped market by introducing and selling shoes.

When the salesmen arrived at their destination, they realized that they were in an impossible situation: all the locals were running around barefooted! An urgent telegram was sent back to the company, informing their boss that there was no market for shoes in that part of the world.

The first batch of salesmen was told to return home, while a new group was sent to tap the 'impossible' market.

When the new salesmen arrived, they were excited by what they saw. "Fantastic market," they wrote back.

What I am trying to say here is that there was no intention to confuse or dishearten readers with those early columns. If you take the knowledge in a positive frame of mind rather than a negative one, then you have nothing to lose.

If you are feeling pain in your arm, you can either try to bear with it if it is within your threshold of pain, or take pain-killers. But the pain will only come back when the tranquilizer wears off.

So the most sensible thing to do is to acknowledge that you are feeling pain, and do something about the source of the pain rather than ignoring it or trying to suppress it. Many people opt for the latter two, until it is too late.

A feng shui man never causes problems when he sees people today living out of harmony with nature because of their ignorance. He just points out the problem—and then gets the blame. The layman should, instead try to find out more about the problem either by himself or by engaging the services of a professional.

When you have a headache, it may be enough to take a tablet and let the pain fade. But if it persists, then it is best to see a doctor rather than swallow 10 or 15 pills at once.

When selling insurance, a salesman may try to convince his customer that his product may be of benefit if the insured party fails to fulfil his earthly obligations to his dependents. The potential buyer may scowl at the salesman for stirring up trouble. Then, with a stroke of the pen, he seals his fate on the dotted line.

The strange thing is that people do not want to know the ultimate truth, that as long as they live, their bodies will deteriorate and finally die. Death owes no favour to anyone, regardless of age.

"But it is always better to face reality than to ignore its existence."

Sometimes, I wonder what will happen when a married man dies and leaves behind his wife and children. Who will put the bread on the table? Who will pay for the children's education and clothing? Who will pay the rent or mortgage?

A dead man has no responsibilities, but leaves behind a trail of problems for others to solve. That is a fact of life. When an insurance salesman points out that death is imminent, he is doing a noble job in telling the truth and offering some form of solution. Sometimes, he may get the boot from customers who do not want to believe in their mortality.

As every man has freedom of choice in a free country, he may exercise this right to make the decision that he feels will suit him best. But it is always better to face reality than to ignore its existence.

The parable of happiness

I AM STAYING on the first floor of a three-storey flat. On the opposite side of the flat is a house with a pointed roof which faces my unit. Friends tell me that the location is bad. Since moving in, I have been experiencing happy and sad moods. Can you please give me some advice on how to overcome the problem?

Jackie Tye
Penang

IT IS TRUE to a certain extent that the pointed roof may have some negative effect on the flats. However, you must not let this trivial point upset you.

But geomancers don't base their pronouncements on just one factor of a house. Other considerations—like the position and design—have to be weighed before a conclusive decision can be made. I suggest you sit tight and hang a *pakua* to reflect the sharp point roof. It may just do the trick.

You have also stated that sometimes you feel very happy and at times very sad. This is part of life. Life is not as complicated as we think it should be unless we make it so by getting entangled in our own web of ignorance.

A Grand Master of philosophy in China once tried very hard to explain the earthly meaning of life to his favourite disciple nicknamed "Butterfly".

Negative feedback from Butterfly told the wise man that he was not making any headway. Thus a different technique had to be used instead and so the master began to spin his philosophy in the form of a short story of why people have to go through a life of tears and joy:

In a remote part of China lies a very poor village where time has almost stood still. The inhabitants go about their daily business in a lackadaisical manner.

Early one morning, a resident was rudely awaken by consistent loud knocks on the front door. The owner of the house unlocked the door and was confronted by a woman. She was the most beautiful woman he had ever set his eyes on. After regaining his composure, he asked the woman the reason of her visit.

She only gave him a lovely smile and then in a sweet voice proclaimed, "I am the Goddess of Light. Whoever welcomes me into his home will be blessed with health, wealth and happiness. I will also banish all ills that pain so many, and mankind will never die if they receive me."

"The truth of life has to be understood if one were to get through it with less pain."

The owner of the house could hardly believe his luck. He invited her into his home. At the presence of this beautiful exalted lady, time was distorted. From the early dawn, noon came all too quickly, followed by the impatient evening as if it could not wait to carry out its nightly duties.

Then came a heavy pounding on the door. He paid no heed, but the sound grew louder. As the owner of the house opened the door, he could only gasp in horror. Before him was a most ugly sight: even though the deep darkness surrounded the evening, a figure of a very ugly, bent woman with torn clothes that could barely covered her old fragile body came into view.

Before the man could ask her who she was, she proclaimed with her deep, croaking voice, "I am the Goddess of Darkness and whoever allows me into his home shall suffer the curse of bad luck and misfortune."

"I bring death and illness to families and now that I must be permitted to enter your house," she insisted strongly.

The owner of the house gripped the edge of the door with the intention of slamming it shut. But before he could act, the Lady of Light spoke. Inquiring about the commotion, she moved to the doorway and surprised the owner of the house by saying that he cannot turn the Goddess of Darkness away.

"We are sisters and we always travel together. In all my journey I preceded her and like a shadow, she will always follow not far behind. Those who accept me into their homes must also allow my sister the same liberty."

The man then thanked both of them for their offers they had intended to shower upon him. He politely refused both his hospitality.

Thus, Butterfly's master ended his story. The truth of life has to be understood if one were to get through it with less pain. We must be able to accept the good with the bad.

Don't blame it on feng shui

THE HOUSE I am living in has a lamp-post across the road that faces the edge of the main door. But when you look from the inside of the house the lamp-post seems to give the impression that it is aligned in the centre of the door.

I am 36 years old and I have been living in this house for 27 years. At present, I am jobless. My father passed away when I was 17 and my mother had a mental breakdown in 1981.

My relationship with my family is also not very good. Your advice would be greatly appreciated.

YKL
Kuala Lumpur

THE LAMP-POST BEING aligned with the main door of your house has little effect on the fend shui of your home.

In Hong Kong, where feng shui is widely practiced, there was once a businessman who siphoned off his own company funds to support his gambling habit and then blamed feng shui for his company's failure.

Similarly, you should not try to pin the blame on the lamp-post alone simple because it "seems" to bisect your door because more often then not, the perception is erroneous.

You have at least 19 years to do something in life before you reach the normal retirement age of 55. When a country like ours is having a booming economy I believe that you should be in the thick of the action, getting a piece of the pie before it is too late. If you keep yourself busy with work, your idle mind will not be put to work by the devil. You will realize how much better it is to pass the time constructively.

As for harmony with your family, I believe that if you begin to assume your responsibility as protector and breadwinner, then things will be much better with them.

Windfall

I HAVE CONSULTED two feng shui masters about my house. Each time both of them remarked that my house has good feng shui but there is one element missing—water. To balance the forces, I was asked to place a pail of water along the entrance as a symbol for wealth.

But whenever my husband and I buy 4D, we always fail to strike the numbers in proper sequence. Can you please advise?

Madam Ling
Kajang

MANY PEOPLE EXPECT goodies to fall into their laps immediately after consulting a feng shui expert and doing as he instructs. Some even have a yardstick in their mind by which they plan to measure the returns they receive.

For instance, there was once a client who set up his own business after consulting a geomancer. A year later, when the feng shui man crossed paths with the entrepreneur, he asked how his business was going. The client said it was good, but not as good as he expected.

Well, new businesses take some time to breakeven, and here was a client who had made money but still complained.

You must remember that when you consult a feng shui expert for your own house or office, you are only trying to balance your own life with the forces of nature around you. You must still work for a living and allow the positive elements to get to work in their own mysteriously ways.

Beyond science and logic

YOUR ARTICLES ON feng shui only encourage superstition. I believe feng shui has no logic behind it as it is no more than an ancient swindle. If feng shui has any truth to it, why can't it be proven scientifically the way acupuncture has been proven?

Science Fan
Prai

FIVE HUNDRED YEARS ago, the world was believed to be flat. Those who dared to venture beyond the horizon of the ocean were deemed foolish. The establishment at that time also declared that the earth was the centre of the universe and that the sun revolved around it.

Nicholes Copernicus, however, was a man ahead of his times and he propounded the theory that the sun is the central body around which the earth and several other planets revolved.

Unfortunately, he could not support this theory with empirical evidence. The authorities saw to it that he was kicked out of the academic circles and even threatened him with imprisonment unless he retracted his "heretical" theory.

But a fact would always remain a fact. Today, we know that Copernicus has been right all a long. Just because there is no instrument to measure feng shui does not prove that it does not exist.

Chinese "secret knowledge" is indeed ancient. In the olden days, such knowledge is jealously guarded. A *sifu* (master) would never teach his disciples everything he knew. He always kept a 'trump card' to protect himself, in the eventuality of challenges against his supremacy.

Thus, as generations passed, the knowledge handed down became less and less; what we now possess is only the crumbs of those ancient secret knowledge.

Acupuncture has been practised by the Chinese for more than two thousand years. Instead of using needles, small sharp stones known as *bian* were used to press vital points in the body to harmonize the flow of *chi* in the body. Only recently has acupuncture been accepted by the West as a alternative medicine.

Scientifically, one cannot measure or see the flow of *chi* travelling through the body as there are no instruments sensitive enough to do the job yet. However, if one recognizes acupuncture, one certainly has to recognize *chi*. Otherwise, one does not know what the subject is all about. And if one recognizes *chi*, feng shui needs no explanation.

As far as feng shui is concerned, I have had eight years of experience as a professional, having studied the subject for 25 years. And, I have seen people benefit from practising feng shui.

PART
2

Perimeters

Tombstone wall

I HAVE A double-storey corner-lot house in Subang Jaya which is near completion. The house is facing east.

I intend to build a Spanish-type perimeter (tomb perimeter) around the house but after reading your article, I have changed my mind. What type of perimeter would you recommend in order to bring good feng shui to the new house?

T. Xavier
Petaling Jaya

Wrong Style: A Spanish-type perimeter would give the house a bizarre look, especially because Chinese tombstones are made with such designs.

THE EAST IS a good direction, provided there are no obstacles in front to create a blockage for you to benefit from the good fortune.

As Asians, we should align our thoughts with the Asian ways as much as possible. I am not criticizing Spanish designs but merely reject it when asked by my clients.

Just imagine the bizarre look of a house with such a perimeter in the evening, with a pale light—spilling out from the hall or other room inside—shining from within. Those with active imaginations would conjure up their minds, a picture of vampires and ghosts. This is not hard to imagine because Chinese tombstones are built with such designs. The pale light is commonly associated with the ghosts and spirit as seen in so many horror movies and television shows.

To be on the safe side, a conventional perimeter will do when you are not consulting a professional geomancer on the matter.

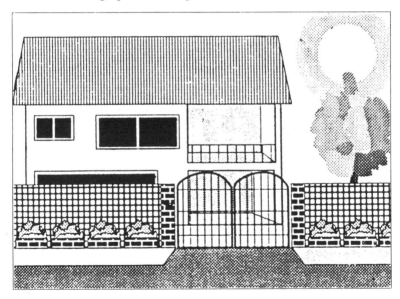

Right Style: It is better to have a conventional perimeter if you are not consulting a professional geomancer.

Hedge of tea-leaves

TEOH CHONG KEE from Malacca has written in to ask about the significance of a hedge of tea leaves, which is rather thick, in front of the main entrance to a house. He wants to know if the hedge has any effect on the general well-being of the occupants of the house.

As far as the Chinese are concerned, tea has never been an obnoxious subject. Instead for generations, the Chinese have often taken along with their breakfast or *dim sum*. It 'washes away' the oil form our eaten food and to a certain extent, helps to clean the internal system.

Recent scientific analysis of tea shows that it has some 20 amino acids, 30 polypeptide bodies, 12 sugars, six organic acids and caffeine and theophylline. The last one is an active ingredient in relaxing the bronchioles of the lungs and also helps in producing urine and stomach acid. It also has fluoride, vitamins C and B complex, and nicotinic acid. This confirms the value of tea.

When tea has been taken as a therapeutic drink for thousands of years, it exact roots and discovery are often shrouded in the mists of time, told only in the form of myths and legends.

One story tells of three travellers making their way to another province in China. In the old days, most people—except the rich, who would ride—had to walk. After some time the men would take a break upon finding a shady place to rest, taking a drink to quench their thirst, or having a meal to fortify them for the long journey ahead.

It so happened that, during such a rest one of them left a pot of water boiling under a tree. After a short nap, they woke up almost at the same time to a strong, mysterious aroma in the air.

They eventually traced the scent to their boiling pot. The rising steam from the pot or some passing wind must have caused some leaves from the tree to fall into the water.

Instead of boiling another pot of water, the men decided to taste this "coloured drink" because they were too thirsty. Cautiously, they tasted it. It proved to be soothing, so they drank some more.

That is how tea was discovered, at least according to this particular story. Whether or not it is true is irrelevant, as the story is told repeatedly and handed down across the generations.

Another version of the discovery of tea is a sad one. It tells of a wandering Buddhist monk who travelled from India to China in the sixth century. He wanted to spread Buddhism to Emperor Liang Wu, who unfortunately did not take a liking to his philosophy. Sadly, the monk retreated to a Shaolin temple in Genan Province. He vowed that, as penance, he would not sleep for several years.

This is quite an impossible task for any man, for sheer exhaustion will overcome the strongest of wills. But this ascetic monk did the impossible; he ordered a disciple to cut out his eyelids with a knife and without eyelids, he could be assured that his eyes would not close in sleep.

As the story goes, a tea plant sprouted from the ground at the spot where his eyelids had fallen. The eyelids symbolize the shedding of tears, and the sadness of the monk who had failed in his mission. This is also why tea has a bitter taste.

You can sometimes see this monk sculpted in miniature bone or wood carvings. His eyes always seem to bulge out of their sockets, but not through any error on the sculptors or carvers' part. This monk in fact, is the famous founder of Zen Buddhism—Bodhidarma, or Da Mo (AD483–540).

Since we have been beating around the tea bush for so long, let's come back to Mr Teoh's original problem: the question of whether a hedge of tea-leaves has any effect on the general well-being of the occupants. We have elaborated on the good points of tea; therefore, the answer is a big no.

Spiked fence

I AM LIVING in a house that faces a bungalow with a fiery perimeter— which also has metal "arrows" bent at angle and pointing directly at my house. I understand that the occupants of my house would not only face "many quarrels and misunderstandings" as you wrote, but also financial problems.

I would therefore appreciate it very much if you would kindly advise me on ways (planting trees, putting up walls, etc.) to prevent such negative chi from affecting my family.

I would of course, upon reading your advice, try to convince the occupants of the bungalow to dismantle their fiery perimeter.

Worried
Malacca

DEAR "WORRIED", TO have a house facing the fiery perimeter of a neighbour's fence will only bring disharmony to the occupants. When we say "disharmony", we mean that every aspect of life that has been upset.

From the financial aspect, you will find it hard to accumulate wealth and money. If you are a businessman, your business will face many uncertainties. A family living in such conditions will also experience frequent quarrels and misunderstandings. As for health-wise, you may find it deteriorating.

The suggested actions that you can take are illustrated in the four diagrams below.

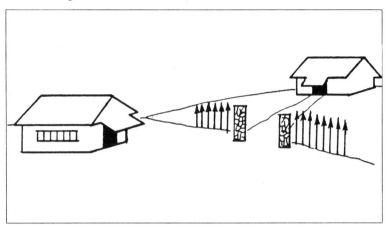

One, talk to your neighbour about his fiery perimeter which has affected your family. He may have put it up simply to discourage thieves from climbing over the fence, with no knowledge whatsoever of the negative influence it would have from feng shui's point of view. If he understands your problem, then simply convince him to bend the sharp points of his fence upright.

Two, if and when talk or negotiations fail, and you are left with no choice, then you should take action on your own (see below).

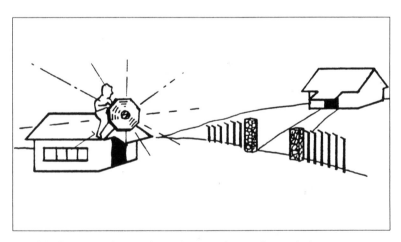

(a) The mysterious *pakua*, when used properly, can help to deflect the bad *chi* coming from the house across the road.

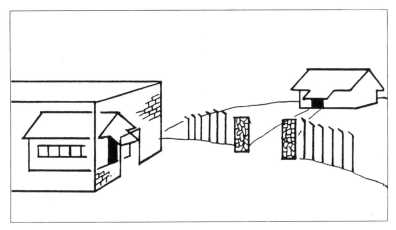

(b) If you intend to build a wall, which may be the next best thing to do, make sure that the top of the wall is higher than the angled points on your opposite neighbour's fence.

There might be some disadvantages, however, if your wall is too high. Wind and *chi* may find it hard to circulate, and bypass your house and compound, thereby depriving you and your family of their benefits.

(c) Planting trees also helps. As young trees take a long time to grow big, you may be left unprotected for the time being. Whether you can withstand the fiery perimeter while the trees grow to maturity remains to be seen. It may be risky to try this method if you do not have the time or strength to face up to the fiery perimeter.

29

Water gate

WE HAVE A letter from Alan Lee and Yap who have sent us a drawing of their double-storey house.

Well, gentlemen, the house is facing east, which is a good direction. But having a gate with a wave-like pattern symbolizes a Water Gate which, being placed at the front of your house, may result in your fortune being siphoned out!

The only way out in this kind of situation is to change your gate design to a more conventional one.

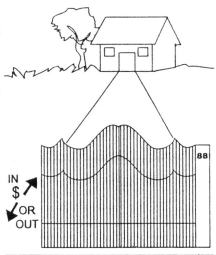

It is unwise to instal a gate with wave-like patterns at the front exit (above). For correction, change it to a more conventional one.

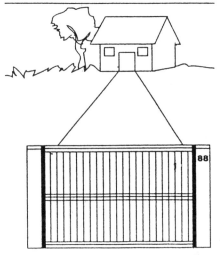

Gates of reverse fortune

MY HOUSE SITS on a rectangular plot of land. It faces the east, and is on higher ground than the opposite house. It is numbered 8. The grilles on the perimeter wall and the main gate bear the "reverse fortune" design. However, the grilles on the doors and windows of the house are of diamond design.

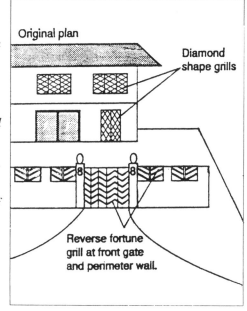

Original plan

Diamond shape grills

Reverse fortune grill at front gate and perimeter wall.

Should I change the patterns of the "reverse fortune" grille the other way round to enhance the feng shui on my house?

Mrs Chin
Penang

A HOUSE LIKE your with the number '8' (*fatt*), which sits on a rectangular piece of land facing the east (Dragon's direction) can only enhance its own feng shui. However, the wrong designs here and there can somewhat undermine the good feng shui that you enjoy.

Yes, you can enhance balance and harmony by changing your grills to that of the "achievers grille".

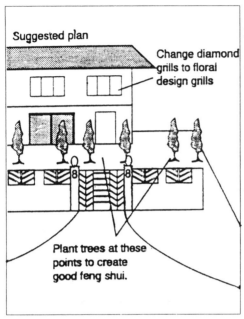

Suggested plan

Change diamond grills to floral design grills

Plant trees at these points to create good feng shui.

Another option is to plant trees where the 'stalks' of the reverse fortune grille would end up like branches growing in an upward trend.

As for the window and door grilles of your house, you might want to change them to a floral design for maximum harmony to bring in more luck.

Grow a hedge

MY PARENTS HAVE been staying in this rented house for the past seven years. We have a nasty neighbour who creates lots of trouble for us, and we have not had any peace of mind since we moved here. Is there anything wrong with the feng shui of my house?

Fifteen-year old girl
Kuala Lumpur

YOUR HOUSE SHOWS that the main door and the back door runs in a straight line. The swift flow of *chi* right through your house can cause disharmony and quarrels to break out.

Since this is a rented house, it is not possible to carry out any renovations. As a temporary measure, place a wind-chime at the main door to slow down the violent *chi*.

You might want to talk to your neighbour and find out why they are so angry with your family. Has your family done anything to make them hoping mad? If so, try to make peace then.

Or you can use reverse psychology by being friendly to your neighbour. In the beginning, they may be confused. But over a period of time, they may sense your sincerity and become friendlier too.

If all else fails, then you might want to move elsewhere to stay. But if for some reason you are unable to shift to another place, and your neighbour is still a pain in the neck, grow a thick hedge to separate the two houses.

Two main gates

I WISH TO construct a small gate next to my main gate for the entry of cars. Please advise.

Mary Chew
Klang

A SMALL HOUSE cannot take two main gates because of the strong current of *chi* which they attract. However, if you find it convenient to make a second entrance, control the rush of *chi* by placing a wall in front of your glass doors.

You may install windows to let sunlight into your house.

Front with a mouth

MY HOUSE HAS very little land in the front and a lot at the back. The building is aligned according to the shape of the land.

Madam P.C. Kok
Kuala Lumpur

A HOUSE LIKE that is considered out of balance. You will not receive enough good things in life as a result of the 'small front'.

To rectify the situation, create a C-shaped mosaic pavement in the front yard. By doing so, you are creating a mouth which can 'gobble up' good things which come your way.

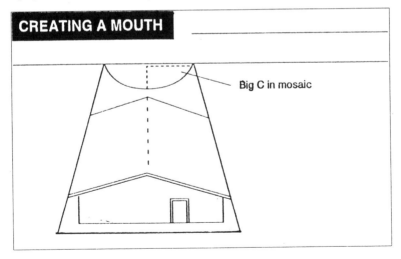

CREATING A MOUTH

Big C in mosaic

PART
3

Windows

Net

Trapped behind the net

INSTEAD OF CHANGING or dismantling iron grilles with net designs, is there another way of creating a harmonious atmosphere in one's house?

Mrs Veronica D.R.
Ipoh

AS NET GRILLES 'imprison' the occupants of the house, the best solution, of course, would be to dismantle the grilles. This can be done, if one is willing to foot the bill. If however, this is not possible, then one way to nullify the adverse effects on feng shui is to hang a pair of steel scissors tied with a red string on top of the net grille. Symbols play an important role in feng shui and here the scissors can help by 'cutting' through the net.

A word of caution though: the scissors should be placed well out of children's reach, to avoid any nasty accidents.

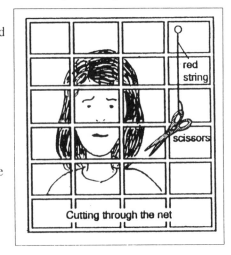

red string

scissors

Cutting through the net

Aerial

MY HOUSE FACES the four windows at the side of another house. In addition to that, a TV antenna sticks out from the roof of that house. What are the effects of all these on my house?

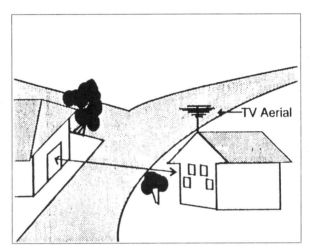

Mrs Chew

AS THE FOUR windows are not totally aligned in straight row facing the main door of your house, you need not worry about the negative influences.

The TV antenna is also too highly placed to affect the feng shui of your house.

PART
4

Numbers

Unlucky house number

MY HOUSE NUMBER is 4, and I share a T-junction with a neighbour. The garden of the house slopes down towards the driveway. Can you explain what effect feng shui has on my house?

L.C. Tan
Kuala Lumpur

TO HAVE A house with the number 4 is but one negative factor to be considered. In fact, numbers did not play an important part in the practice of feng shui until recently.

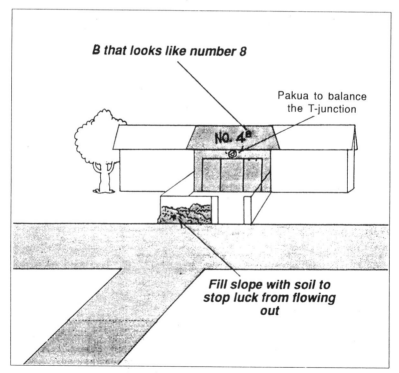

B that looks like number 8

Pakua to balance
the T-junction

NO. 4ᴮ

Fill slope with soil to
stop luck from flowing
out

The use of numbers can be traced to the growing population, followed by the increase in homes and vehicles. Numbers become a source of convenience in this growing tangle of homes and cars, and slowly numbers began to be accepted in feng shui.

Modern Chinese, especially the Cantonese, always try not to associate themselves with the number 4 because when spoken, it means death. So most of the time, the number is avoided. In the practice of feng shui, the number 4 need not necessarily mean death, but could also mean a stopover or transition from one's present position. If you are looking for advancement in your job or business, it may be delayed.

As a solution you can add a small B besides the number 4 making it look like 4^B. The letter B may be made to look like the figure 8, which means prosperity. When you have 4^B, it means "always prosperous." The only catch is that you have to take the risk of the postman being confused when he comes to deliver your mail!

As your house garden also slopes down towards the driveway, it simple means your luck will also flow away. With the T-junction you face, you may be doubly unlucky in your endeavours. To minimize the imbalance of your feng shui, simply fill up your garden slope to make it flat. As for the T-junction, put up a *pakua* to balance the forces for the time being.

Later, when you have enough money, it may be a good idea to move.

Number 4

AFTER BUYING A house, a friend of mine found that he had been allotted house No. 4, which is considered a bad number amongst the Chinese. What he did was remove the numeral 4 from his house and replace it with the word "FOUR".

Does this action have any effect in solving the problem of bad feng shui?

House No. 3
Petaling Jaya

THE NUMBER 4 (*sei*) is the sound of death when spoken in Cantonese. So by changing the numeral 4 to the word "FOUR", he may end up buying a sound of "fire". If the occupants of the house are sensitive character-wise, the word FOUR may add

extra 'fuel'. In the end, they end up with lots of quarrels and misunderstandings.

The word FOUR may be used in more positive manner if the occupant and his family find themselves lacking courage in facing their daily lives. As the word has the 'sound of fire', it certainly may lend them some spirit, giving them the courage to face life in a more positive way each day.

Having to choose between the numeral 4 and word FOUR is like being caught between the devil and the deep blue sea. You have to choose the one that will affect you more positively.

The other point the house-owner must take into consideration is that, if he happens to use the word FOUR instead, his mailman may overlook his house!

Bad luck number 8

WE BOUGHT A house eight years ago with our hard-earned savings. Since then, our financial situation has gotten from bad to worse. We seemed to be dogged by ill luck. Even before we moved into the house, our neighbours had warned us that the house brought bad luck to its occupants. But we ignored their advice. Today, we suffer the consequences. Is there anything I can do to improve the situation? My house number is 8.

Anxious Resident
Taiping

THE NUMBER "8" normally augurs well for the occupants as it signifies prosperity. But when it comes to feng shui, this need not necessarily be so, as other factors have to be taken into consideration too.

The sketch of your house shows that it is facing east or the Green Dragon Area. This is a positive point in feng shui. Even though your house may be seem to be in harmony with Nature, we should not forget the internal arrangement. It has to be well balanced too for you to benefit from it.

One of the main reasons for the bad feng shui in your house can be traced to the front door and the master bedroom door. As the door of your master bedroom opens outwards, it clashes with the front door. As there is disturbance at the main entrance, fortune and luck are less likely to flow in. Besides, such clashes are likely to give rise to more family quarrels.

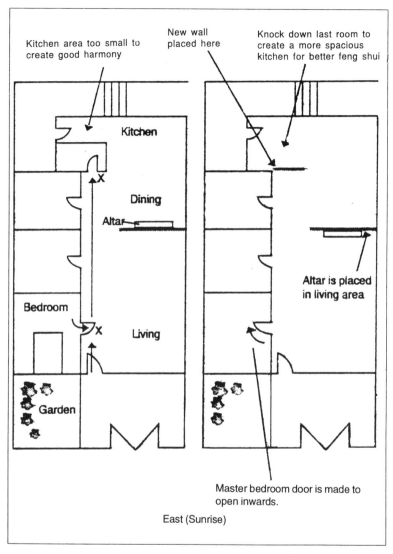

Kitchen area too small to create good harmony

New wall placed here

Knock down last room to create a more spacious kitchen for better feng shui

Kitchen

X

Dining

Altar

Bedroom

X Living

Garden

Altar is placed in living area

Master bedroom door is made to open inwards.

East (Sunrise)

This problem can be easily rectified by changing the master bedroom door so that it opens inwards. The front door of your house also faces a bedroom near the kitchen. When an open door faces another, it is considered bad luck because *chi* is found travelling in a straight line. Besides, a bedroom should never be too near a kitchen otherwise bad health will befall the occupants.

47

The bedroom seems to have been built into the kitchen space, thus making the kitchen smaller and narrower. As the kitchen is a place where food is cooked, by making the kitchen smaller, it signifies that food will be hard to come by.

The only solution then is to knock down the room and place a full-height wall there as shown in the diagram. This should help balance your house and put it back in order.

And finally, one last suggestion: instead of having your alter in the dining area, it would be more appropriate if it is left in the living room facing outwards. It may also be good for you to get someone to bless your house, cleaning it of any past negativeness left by the previous owner.

Number 14

OUR DOUBLE-STOREY INTERMEDIATE lot faces the south. Ever since we shifted into the house, we find it very difficult to save.

Our house number is 14 and the number 4 is placed slightly higher that the number 1 on the letter box. The main entrance has a sliding door which is tinted.

Kindly advise if such a placing is in order.

Khoo L.H.
Petaling Jaya

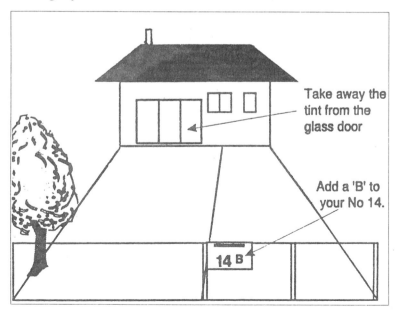

Take away the tint from the glass door

Add a 'B' to your No 14.

14 B

AS NUMBER 14 when pronounced in Cantonese literally means "surely die", many people shy away from that number for their house, cars, etc. However, as you are unfortunate to have the number tagged on to your house, your letter box should not have the 4 placed higher than the number 1 as this would only make the number 4 more significant.

Moreover, your sliding door has a dark tint which would only intensify bad tidings. For better harmony, bring the number 4 down to the same level as number 1. You could write to the relevant authorities to have a small B (to symbolize the number 8 for prosperity) tagged on to number 14. This would give your house a good connotation such as "one would always prosper".

As for the sliding door, simply untint it.

Number 17

I AM STAYING on the ground floor of a three-storey town house. My unit is No. 17, while the unit above is 17A.

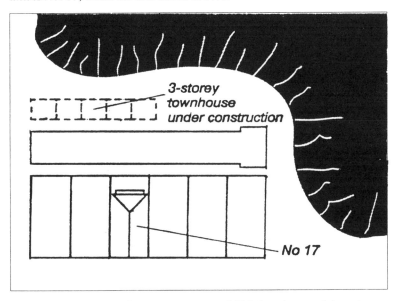

I bought it from a businesswoman in 1991. I understand that she wanted to open a video rental shop on the ground floor. She later changed her mind when she found that it was not a good location.

Can you please comment on the feng shui of my unit?

New House Buyer
Kuala Lumpur

THE 80-FOOT HILL nearby blocks the flow of *chi* to your unit. There's a lot of stagnant air in the vicinity, which can adversely affect one's health. To make matters worse, the dead-end road on the right symbolizes a dead end in one's progress in life.

To bring about balance, plant lots of trees in your compound. This way, more oxygen can be circulated within your house to give you and your family a healthier environment. Place a small bronze cannon as a symbolic gesture to blast away the obstacles posed by the dead-end road and the hill.

Number 18

ALTHOUGH WE LIVE in a house bearing the number 18, none of the occupants seem to enjoy good luck. In fact, we have been bugged by various illness and failures.
The house that we live in is the narrowest in the row of seven houses.

M.K. Cheah
Penang

THE HOUSE NUMBER is only one of the criteria that a geomancer looks at in assessing the feng shui of a house.

From your explanation that there are seven houses in the same row where your house is the smallest and is caught in the middle, I would say that your luck is being squeezed out. It is better for you to vacate the premises and look for another place to stay.

Number 24

*I LIVE IN A double-storey house bearing the number 24. It faces the
south. I have placed a pakua at the main door, as my house faces higher
ground. Inside, the main entrance and staircase run in a straight line.
As a recourse, I have placed a screen in between them.*
Is there any way I can improve the feng shui of my house?

Feng shui Seeker

THE NUMBER 24 literally means "easy to die" when pronounced in
Cantonese. As such, it is an ominous number for a house. So the
occupant may find his career coming to an abrupt end, especially when
the staircase is aligned with the main entrance to symbolize a 'one-way
ticket' out.

It's good that you have placed a screen to cheek the direct flow of
chi, to minimize this adverse effect. South is a good direction to face.
Unfortunately, your house is on lower ground than the house opposite.

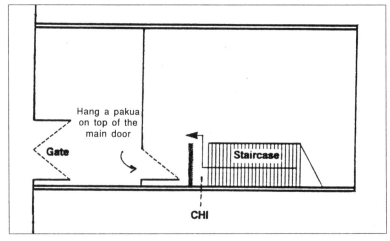

As you have placed a *pakua* on the door, that's about the most you can make of the present situation.

Number 33

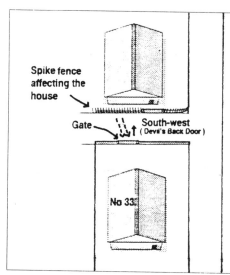

Spike fence affecting the house

Gate

South-west (Devil's Back Door)

No 33

I HAVE JUST moved into a house that faces the south-west. Its number is 33. A spike fence faces the house.
Does this signify something bad?

Chee Kee Chean

YOUR HOUSE NUMBER is 33, or *san-san* in Chinese, which means "double growth".

However, this does not necessarily mean good feng shui when other factors are taken into consideration.

Your house entrance faces the south-west, which in feng shui is considered the Devil's Back Door, that is, a bad direction. Besides that, the spike fence carries *sha chi* in your direction and this

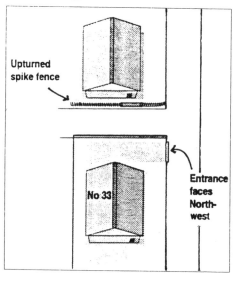

Upturned spike fence

No 33

Entrance faces North-west

also bring bad tidings for you and your family. You could have a word with your neighbour about modifying the shape of his fencing. If diplomacy fails, then a *pakua* would help to deflect the *sha chi*. Your house is on a corner-lot, so it is easier to move the entrance to the north-west.

Number 38

WE BOUGHT A corner-terraced house with the number 38. In front of our house is a big monsoon drain. There is a three-storey high school with its back facing our direction.

Since we moved in, there has always been some stumbling block in the way of my husband's promotion. I reckon my husband is getting nowhere even though he works very hard in the company. Can I place a small mirror in front of my house to improve the situation?

Mrs Y.K. Loong
Klang

THE BACK OF the school and the big tree which blocks your entrance, create obstacles for the occupants of your house. The hump on the road seems to run towards your house, symbolizing a double obstacle for you. As water is seen travelling straight pass your house

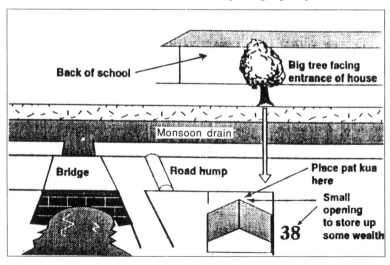

Back of school

Big tree facing entrance of house

Monsoon drain

Bridge

Road hump

Place pat kua here

Small opening to store up some wealth

38

through the big monsoon drain, you may well see financial rewards pass your way.

To offset all these negative effects, place a *pakua* in front of your house to reflect off the negativeness coming from the school, the big tree and the road hump.

You can make a small opening on the figure 8 of your house number 38 so that some water passing parallel through your direction can be stored to give you some financial stability.

Number 43

I HAVE A house facing a hill; my colleagues and friends have told me that this has many negative effects from a feng shui point of view. My house number is 43; a pump-house and reservoir are situated opposite the home. Please advise.

Curious Leoh
Kuala Lumpur

WELL, CURIOUS, THE number of your house is *"sei sang"* (literally, "always surviving") and it faces east with a reservoir (a symbol of money) in sight. This shows you are a very ambitious person.

The setback is that the reservoir is off to the right instead of being directly in front of your house. This causes your home to face the hill, thereby blocking your achievements.

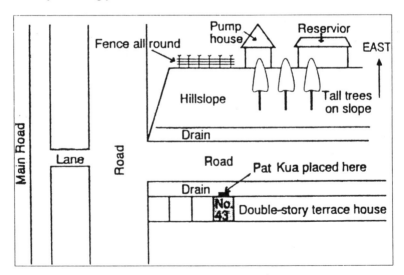

What you can do to neutralize is to place a *pakua* over your door. This ought to improve your situation.

Number 53

I HAVE BOUGHT a house number 53. We are not Cantonese but in Cantonese, the number 53 means "not living". Furthermore, there are two pillars blocking the main entrance. Please advise.

KH
Kuala Lumpur

NUMBERS DO CARRY a degree of significance in feng shui. Whether a person is of a different dialect or race does not matter when he lives in an area where the belief of feng shui is strong. The force of the archetypal symbol will somehow cut across the barriers and make things—good or bad—happen to him.

To neutralize the force of the number 53, you can plant a tree next to your house to signify "life". Place two bamboo flutes in the form of an "X" at the pillars to cross out the blockage at your main entrance.

Number 54

MY HOUSE NUMBER is 54, and it faces the north-east as well as a T-junction. I understand that this is bad feng shui. There are two sewage ponds nearby too. Please advise.

Harry Khoo
Klang

A HOUSE THAT faces a T-junction is deemed unlucky. And if it faces the north-east too, this is considered doubly unlucky for the owner as spirits and ghosts could roam freely into the premises.

Fortunately for you, there is a monsoon drain which separates the T-junction from your house, and absorbs any bad *chi* coming from that direction. Moreover, your house is numbered 54 (*ng sei* in Cantonese means "won't die"). Under such circumstances, your house has created its own 'force-field' to negate any adverse influences coming its way. However, you can add a *pakua* to reinforce its strength. As for the sewage pond, they are too far away to have any significant influence on your house.

Number 66

MY HOUSE IS numbered 66 and faces south. The houses in the back row are on higher ground while those in front are on lower ground. My bathroom, kitchen and main door are aligned.
What is the general feng shui of my house?

Sylvie Hung
Klang

THE POSITIVE POINT of your house is that it is backed up by a strong 'wall' of higher houses and clear of obstacles in the front. The one thing you must take notice of is the number. Sixty-six is translated into *"luk-luk"* in Chinese, which also means "to roll".

Furthermore, the bathroom (which is considered a place where wealth is stored) is directly facing the kitchen and main door. This is courting financial disaster.

To rectify the situation, place a partition between the bathroom and the kitchen door. Renovate your house door to face east, which is an auspicious direction.

PART
5

Hills

Types of hills

READER BENJI CHEONG of Penang wrote in to ask what effects a tall hill will have on the occupants of a house facing it. He says the hill is about 10km from the house.

Before a feng shui expert can give an accurate answer and advice, he must first know the type and shape of the mound. Hills are more than what they seem in geomancy.

The same principle applies when you are buying a car. In choosing a car, you have to consider the make, model, colour, and of course the price. It has been said that all cars have four wheels. But, they don't all cost the same. A certain model may cost an affordable $20,000 to $30,000 while another may cost the earth. Most times, the more expensive model has more features.

Back to hills: when confronted with one, a feng shui expert will have to classify the hill into one of the five categories according to the elements—wood, fire, metal earth and water. Only then can be analyse and determine if the situation is good or bad.

☐ A hill with a conical shape belongs to the fire element. This is because the profile or shape resembles flames.

☐ A concave or hump-shaped mountain or hill represents metal. Just take a look at an inverted wok and you will know why.

☐ A high and steep form with a flat top represents wood as it resembles a tree.

☐ A plateau with a long, flat surface belongs to the earth element as it resembles the palm of a hand.

☐ A ridge with wave-like formation represents water.

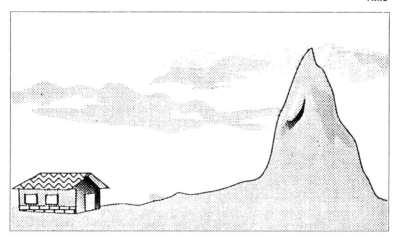

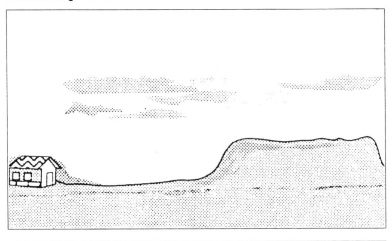

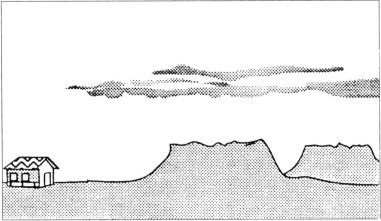

Once you have identified the element the hill belongs to, you can go about analysing the situation. Without a sketch or picture of the shape of the hill, I cannot accurately give you an analysis.

The diagrams provided should give you a rough idea of what element the hill you referred to belongs.

A word of caution when analysing the hill: not all may belong to one element. There are times when a hill may combine a number of elements—fire and wood, metal and water, or wood and earth.

Stopped by a hill

I RECENTLY BOUGHT a house which faces east. It has a small hill with tall trees which overshadow the house. I have come to understand that it is considered bad feng shui to face such surroundings.

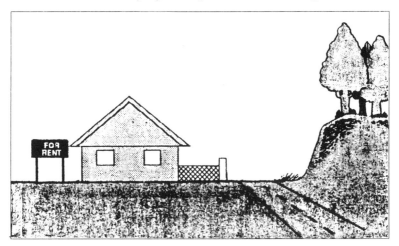

I would like to ask you for advice on how to get around this so-called blockage, for myself and on behalf of my neighbours whose homes face the hill as well.

Danny Leong
Cheras

TO HAVE YOUR house facing east is considered good feng shui as it is the direction of the *loong* (dragon). Having a wooded hill facing your house is another matter. The hill, in fact, acts as a blockage to the good *chi* flowing from the east, thereby depriving you and your family the chance to enjoy its benefits.

It is like having two birds in the bush and none in the hand. One must also understand that a hill is an obstacle in the terminology of feng shui. So, if you are destined for a promotion in your job, or an expansion of your business, and find yourself going nowhere, then it is an indication that your feng shui is being blocked.

You certainly cannot level the hill. The quickest solution would be to move out. Or else, hang a *pakua* over your main door facing the hill.

You may even consider renting out the house and moving somewhere else for the time being. Who knows, in future the hill may indeed be levelled for development purposes and you can return.

Dead end by a hill

WE HAVE BEEN staying in our present house for the past seven years, and ever since we moved in, we have been living a hand-to-mouth existence. Whenever we do get some extra cash, there is bound to be some unforeseen expenditure.

My house is numbered 40, and is a corner lot. The front and side of my house face a 3-meter high ground. Most of the time we enter our house by the side entrance.

Mrs Rajah
Shah Alam

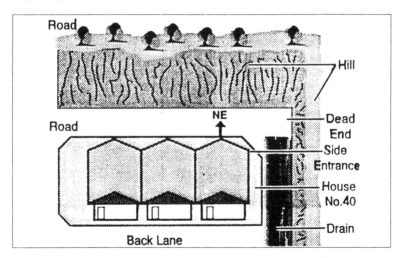

YOUR DIAGRAM SHOWS that your house faces the north-east, which is an unfortunate direction to face. But since you are using the side entrance which is on the south-east, it helps to alleviate the problem. But then your main gate still faces the north-east which is considered the Devil's Door. As your house faces higher grounds on the front and side, this symbolizes a lot of obstacles facing the family, in terms of wealth, health and progress.

Your house number of 40 translates into Cantonese as "*sei*" (dead). To compound the problem, it is at a dead end. Most cul-de-sac houses are not good in terms of feng shui as they can only benefit from the remaining *chi* which comes in after all the other houses lined up in the front have benefited.

In your case, bad luck is intensified as there is a drain which runs parallel to the side of the house and faces your side entrance. This symbolizes wealth being drained off. Even though a *pakua* could be placed at the front and side of the house to deflect the bad *chi* from the high ground, this may or may not work, due to the proximity of the raised land.

Then again, there's the problem of the drain at the side, and being situated at a dead end—these are things which you cannot do anything about. So you can see now that no matter how hard you try, money seems to slip away.

If all else fails, I can only suggest that you move. I am sure that you and your family will find peace and harmony again in a new place.

Rocky hill

MY HOUSE IS located with a row of houses on a hill-slope. Originally, it was supposed to be sited on the highest point, with a view of the city. Unfortunately, due to difficulties encountered during the construction, the row of houses, including mine, are now blocked by the solid rock hill.

I have attached the layout plan, and would appreciate your comments on the feng shui of my house. What precautions can I take to ward off any adverse influences?

Mrs Lee
Kuala Lumpur

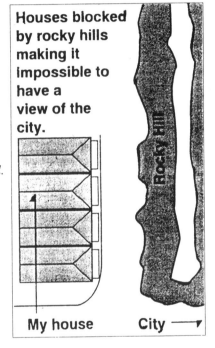

Houses blocked by rocky hills making it impossible to have a view of the city.

My house　　　**City** ⟶

SINCE YOU HAVE already bought your house, there is little you can do about the situation. You can expect to make little progress with the rock outcrop blocking your house. As a temporary measure, you can place a *pakua* in front of your house.

PART
6

Fire-Hydrants

Fronting house

MY HOUSE FACES a fire-hydrant. Is there a way to prevent misfortune?

Charlie Yew

YOU ARE INDEED lucky to have a fire-hydrant across the road from your house. Compared to having a giant 'dumpster', bus-stop or huge tree, the hydrant can be 'exploited' to play a more positive role in your home's feng shui.

A fire-hydrant is also a source of *sui* (money), but it has a different meaning when separated by a road. The road creates a barrier, which means that water can be seen but is unattainable.

Since it is not possible to move the hydrant, why not do the obvious? Hang a large mirror on one wall to reflect the image of the hydrant from outside. By creating an image of the hydrant in the intended place you have indirectly brought the *sui* into your home.

The real hydrant is outside. Not here.

Mirror

Running straight through

A FIRE-HYDRANT SITS right in front of the entrance to my clinic. From my experience, I think it is bad feng shui.

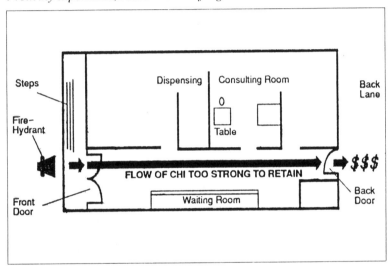

What can I do correct it? I can ask the Fire Department to remove the hydrant to the side of the building if it will help.

Dr Bala
Klang

FROM THE LAYOUT of the clinic supplied, it would seem that you have double trouble. Firstly, the hydrant acts as an obstruction to good feng shui. Secondly, *sui* (water or money) from the hydrant flows in through the front door and directly out through the back exit.

This means you may make a lot of money from your practice but due to unforeseen circumstances or prior commitments, you are left with little profit at the end of the day. Thus, money comes easily and is spent just as quickly.

Asking the Fire Services Department to move the fire-hydrant to the corner of the block will help. An immediately remedy would be to deflect the bad feng shui. To prevent your earnings and health from being siphoned away, you can realign the position of your back door to one corner so that it is not directly facing the entrance. At the same time, get a mirror or *pakua* to reflect the hydrant.

With these changes, you will definitely see some profit by the end of your clinic's financial year.

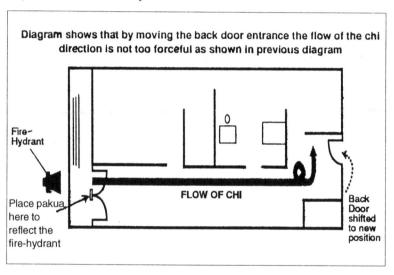

Diagram shows that by moving the back door entrance the flow of the chi direction is not too forceful as shown in previous diagram

Fire-
Hydrant

Place pakua here to reflect the fire-hydrant

FLOW OF CHI

Back Door shifted to new position

Hydrant-thief

MY HOUSE FACES the east. Can you tell me whether it is a positive sign to have a fire-hydrant at a corner outside the house?

Lee Kok Kiong
Kedah

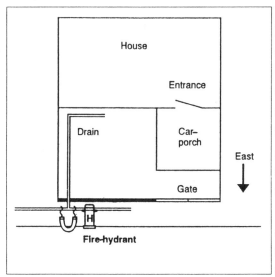

WHILE YOUR HOUSE may be collecting good *chi* coming from the east, wealth will be siphoned away by the drain in the garden which is almost aligned with the hydrant.

The hydrant acts like a strong magnet which attracts its own elements. As water is a symbol of money, the hydrant will exert its influence in drawing money away from your house.

You can reverse this situation by reconstructing that stretch of the drain so that it slopes inwards towards the house. This also means that you have to extend the drain so that it runs along the front of the house, with an outlet which opens out on the other end of the house.

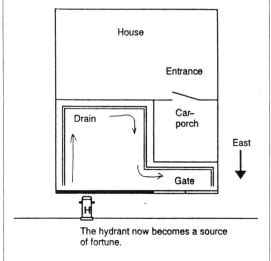

House

Entrance

Drain

Car-porch

East

Gate

H

The hydrant now becomes a source of fortune.

The hydrant will now become a source of wealth, since the drain starts there, and the water which runs along the front of your house will bring about harmony in your family as well as a sound bank account!

Hydrant at the
side lane

E.L. OOI of Penang, wants to know the feng shui of his house (No. 23) which has a fire-hydrant just beside it.

The interpretation of a fire-hydrant's effect on the feng shui of a house can either be positive or negative, depending on its placement.

As for your house, the hydrant, which is beside the fence and by a lane, signifies that money is 'running away' without being checked or collected.

The number of your house, 23, denotes 'easy living'. But with the hydrant acting adversely on the feng shui, its meaning could easily change to 'easy money, easy go'.

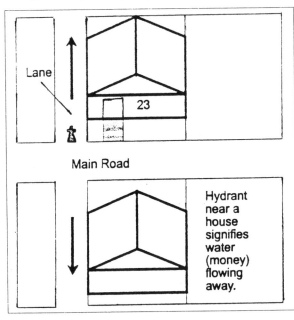

Lane

23

Main Road

Hydrant near a house signifies water (money) flowing away.

There is actually nothing much you can do about it since both the hydrant and lane are government property. However, by putting up a reflective mirror on one wall of your

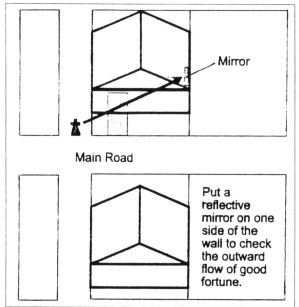

house, you could check the outward 'flow' of your good fortune.

Mirror

Main Road

Put a reflective mirror on one side of the wall to check the outward flow of good fortune.

Sharing a hydrant

THERE IS A fire-hydrant outside my neighbour's house while the drain in my compound is covered with pave bricks. What is your opinion on this?

Mrs Y. H. Kim
Petaling Jaya

IT DOES NOT matter whether your drain is covered or otherwise. If it flows towards the hydrant, your wealth is flowing away. However, since the hydrant is nearer to your neighbour's house, both of you are sharing the same amount of wealth.

If you want to gain an advantage, divert your drain to flow away from the hydrant.

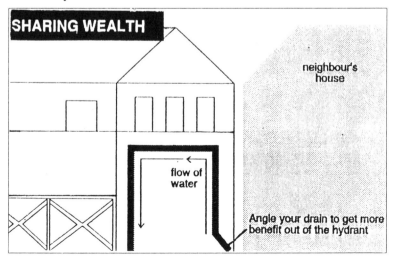

SHARING WEALTH

neighbour's house

flow of water

Angle your drain to get more benefit out of the hydrant

PART
7

Water-Tanks

Fronting

A YEAR AGO, my wife bought a single-storey terraced house in Johor Baru. We moved in recently. At present, I am working in Kuala Lumpur and go back to Johor Baru twice a month.

My house number is 15. Recently, I discovered that my house actually faces a big water-tank and is 'bracketed' by two air-wells of the water-tank.

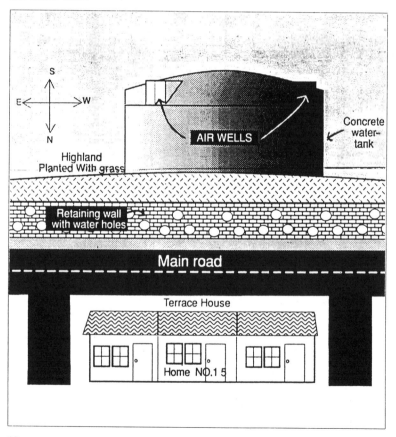

What are the implications of this sort of positioning in feng shui terms?

Michael Low
Selangor

THE DIRECTION OF your house, which faces south, is considered an auspicious direction; it is also known as the Phoenix direction. Your house, being sandwiched by your neighbour's houses (from the diagram you included) has proper balance. Across your house, the two air-wells also provide a 'balance'.

Finally, to have a huge water-tank facing your house with a retaining wall and its drainage holes, is considered good feng shui. Water flowing towards your house symbolizes money flowing in your direction.

To maximize this effect, perhaps you could cause the tail of the '5' in your house number, 15, to curl up a little more, making it resemble '6'. In Chinese, 16 means 'forever rolling'.

With this and the combination of the above-mentioned points, you and your family could forever be "rolling in dough", as they say.

Trident

I WOULD LIKE to seek your advice on the feng shui of my home, a double-storey terraced house that faces west. A big steel water-tank is found opposite. A house nearby also has its main entrance aligned with mine, with a pakua and a three-pronged steel piece hanging on top.

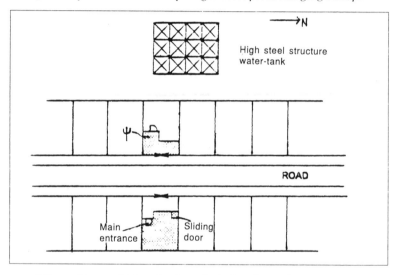

All my elders said that the feng shui of my house is negative. Please help.

T.T. Low
Kepong

HAVING A WATER-TANK in front of your house would normally be considered favourable because water symbolizes wealth. But to have your house facing west, which is not considered a very good direction, cancels out this positive element.

To lessen the intensity of this, it is best to change the door's facing to the south, if possible.

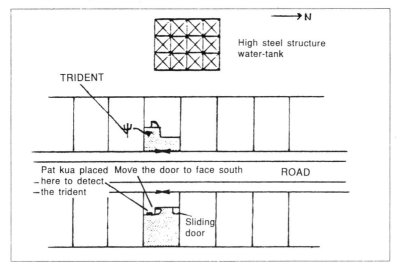

As for the three-pronged steel piece affixed to the *pakua* over your neighbour's door, it is known as a trident. If it is pointing straight at your house, it would only bring ill luck.

What you could do is try talking to your neighbour. If diplomacy fails then put a *pakua* over your own door to counter it.

Fronting reservoir

WE HAVE BEEN staying in our double-storey house for the past eight years. Our house faces the sunset. Just across the road is a small hill with a reservoir on the right.

Is this bad feng shui for my house, and if so, how can I rectify the situation?

Chui
Kuala Lumpur

A RESERVOIR SYMBOLIZES wealth, but in your case, as your house also faces the sunset, it signifies a downward trend in your financial situation. A *pakua* is not applicable here as it would reflect away your wealth, and make matters worse.

What you can do is to put a mirror on the top of your side door as the reservoir is in that direction, to attract wealth into the house.

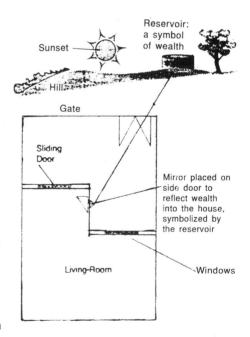

Sunset

Reservoir: a symbol of wealth

Hill

Gate

Sliding Door

Mirror placed on side door to reflect wealth into the house, symbolized by the reservoir

Living-Room

Windows

PART
8

Water

Fish-pond

MRS CINDY FOO of Petaling Jaya says her husband intends to rear some Japanese carp in the house compound. She would rather have the artificial pond built on the balcony just above the car-porch than in the garden. Her house faces north.

Some people rear Japanese carp as a hobby; others do it for its commercial value. Whatever the reason, you should build a pond in the proper place, all in the name of harmony.

The cardinal directions of east and north are safe to build on. The land to the south is considered 'fiery' and because fire and water are incompatible elements, building a pond there is not advisable.

Another thing you should consider is that, once the pond is built, your husband should rear the fish in the following numbers to enhance his luck: six, eight, 16, 18, 19 and 23.

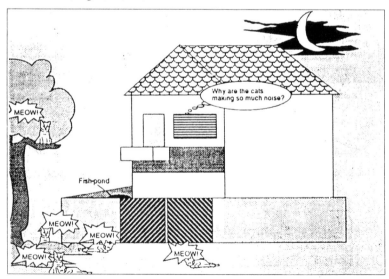

Tap

I WOULD BE much obliged if you could assist me with regard to the feng shui of my house.

I live in a housing estate which consists of over 600 houses. My house itself faces an open field with nothing obvious obstructing its view. However, luck and fortune do not seem to be coming my way. On the contrary, money goes out almost as soon as it comes in.

I wonder if my luck is being obstructed by some other factors, perhaps the pillar or tap in the garden.

L. Wong
Kedah

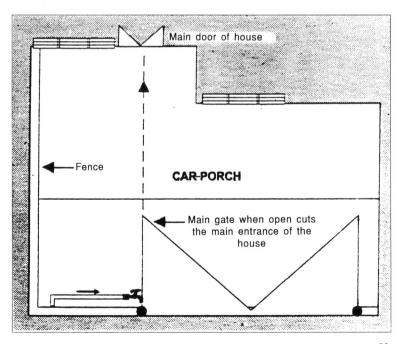

BECAUSE YOUR HOUSE has a free, open field which has no high objects in it to block feng shui, your assumption is correct when you state that the culprit may be the pillar of the main gate. When fully opened, the gate is perpendicular to the main entrance to your house; in fact, it 'cuts' the door, thereby splitting your luck.

What you could do is move the pillar into a position where it will neither obstruct nor 'cut' your door.

The garden tap can also be adjusted so that it is perpendicular to your door, thereby symbolizing lots of *sui* (water) and luck flowing in.

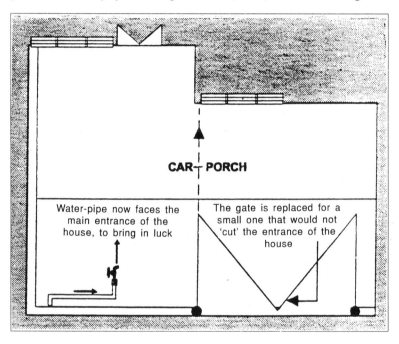

CAR PORCH

Water-pipe now faces the main entrance of the house, to bring in luck

The gate is replaced for a small one that would not 'cut' the entrance of the house

Bad kind of light

CAN YOU TELL me whether it is good to have a drain outlet which faces a lamp-post?

Worried
Muar

A LIGHT IS used to brighten up an area which is too dark for us to see. The light attracts insects which find it warm and fascinating. As most living creatures are attracted to light, we can say that light has a 'magnetic pull'.

For that reason, a lighted lamp-post symbolizes a tool of attraction. To have one's drain outlet facing it is to have one's wealth being siphoned away.

To counter this, you should redirect the flow of water from your house so that the lamp-post is behind, and not in front of, the drain. Cover with a cement slab the portion of the drain at the main entrance. Water should never be seen running out of the house.

Underground culvert

MY HOUSE FACES an underground culvert which drains water off into a nearby river. You have described it in a past column as "money being siphoned off".

Don't ask me to move as I have been staying here for almost 35 years. In my family, we always seem to miss a number here or there in the 4D or 1+3D.

Please advise.

C.T. Loh
Pahang

IN LIFE, SOME people are bestowed with so-called 'gambling luck' but not everyone. Otherwise, if everyone were to win all the time and leave no losers, it would be a disaster for the casinos and others who provide the avenues for gambling.

Assuming that you and your family are gifted with gambling luck, you would still have a very big problem to solve. The diagram you provided shows an underground culvert draining off water. This signifies money being siphoned away, and could be one reason you and your family always seem to 'miss' in 4D.

Your house number is 6, which means rolling. But this is only compounded by the presence of the culvert, as it is so much easier for money to flow away. It would not be easy for your to rectify the problem. By no means can you alter the direction of the culvert, or seal it up (not unless you want to be in serious trouble with the local authorities).

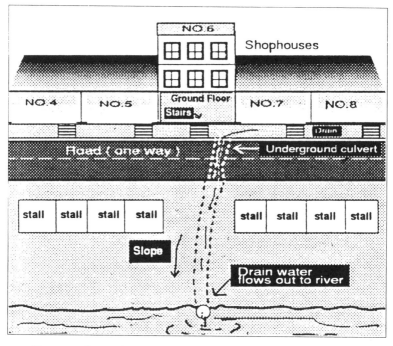

Since you have also said that you will not move out, then I suggest you consult a geomancer near you who will be able to survey the site and recommend something more acceptable to you.

Monsoon drain

WHAT HAPPENS WHEN a house is located in such a way that a big monsoon drain flows along the direction of the main road which faces the house?

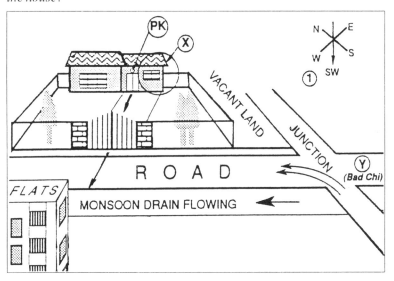

A block of flats also partially blocks the view of the house. What effect will all this have on the occupants?

Cheong Chik Sun
Penang

BY LOOKING AT the drawing you have sent, we would have to analyse it in sections for easy reading.

The positive aspect: Your house sits on a rectangular piece of land, and that is a good thing.

The negative aspects include:

☐ The house faces south-west which is known as the Devil's Door in feng shui; it is not a very good direction to face.

☐ Your front door is in a straight line with the main gate, which also faces south-west. Such an alignment (of door and gate) is considered negative, especially so in this particular direction. The occupants of the house would find their health easily affected.

☐ Your front door and gate, which are already aligned and facing south-west also face a monsoon drain that flows straight along the road. It shows that you can make a lot of money but will not be able to hold on to it for long (it just flows away).

☐ If your house is close to a major junction, make sure that those who are physically or mentally weak should not occupy the rooms marked "X" in the diagram because of the flow of bad *chi* coming from direction "Y".

☐ As we said earlier, the house faces a bad direction. The flats that partially obscure your view do not have a bad effect; in fact they block part of the bad forces coming your way.

The suggested remedies include:

☐ Move your door to face another direction.

☐ Change the facing of your gate, too, if possible.

☐ Place a *pakua* where indicated for further protection from the south-west force.

Master bedroom

Room No.2

Wall that blocks the flow of Chi

W. C.

Ⓧ

Flow of Chi

Kitchen

Main door

Entrance of flat

☐ Plant trees at the corner to take the brunt of the bad *chi* coming from the road junction.

Note that these recommendations are made based on the drawing that you sent in. A professional feng shui man may see things differently if he visits the site. If you are not sure of what to do, get professional help and do not try to do things yourself.

Obstacles to flow

MRS THAM OF Kuala Lumpur intends to buy a single-storey terraced house which is facing west. A narrow stream flows in front of the house, running into a pond. Alongside the stream is a road which leads to other housing estates.

She has sent us a diagram and wants to know what the feng shui of the place is.

House with bad feng shui

Well, it is normally considered bad luck if a house faces west, which is known as the White Tiger.

Furthermore, if a house is situated too close to a dead end, where the flow of *chi* is stopped, then it is considered the 'end of the road' to progress for the owner.

In your case, you are fortunate to have a stream nearby. What you can do to tap the potential good feng shui of your environment is to relocate your main door to face north by making some extensions to your house.

The stream flowing into the pond symbolizes the gathering of wealth, which can now be collected by the new doorway.

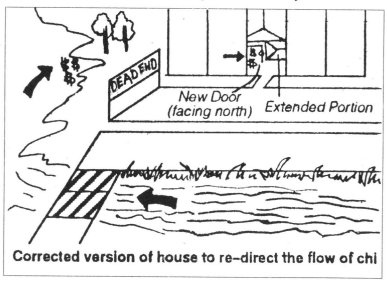

New Door
(facing north)   Extended Portion

Corrected version of house to re-direct the flow of chi

Turning point of river

THE NUMBER OF my house is 26 and it is situated in the middle of a row of nine houses. I have a feeling that the tree, the lamp-post and the temple toilet opposite are blocking my luck.

Fifteen years ago when I moved in, I remember placing a mirror over the main door of my house. Now I cannot remember what happened to it. Can you advise me on the best course of action to take?

Mrs Ng
Penang

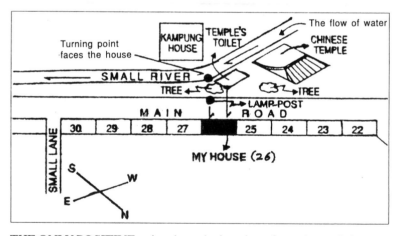

THE ONLY POSITIVE point about the location of your house is its position, that is, being right smack in the middle of the row, which at least gives it some balance.

Your house faces the south-west direction, which is known as the Devil's Back Door. Secondly, the sharp corner of the temple's toilet bisects your house, and this could lead to disharmony among the occupants, bad luck and ill health.

One consolation is the large tree which absorbs part of this bad *chi*. To offset the cutting edge of the toilet, place a *pakua* over your main door. The river coming to a 'turning point' in front of your house is considered bad feng shui because it is said to take your wealth away.

If you really intend a change of fortune, the best solution would be for you to move.

Flow from the Devil's Door

I AM STAYING in a semi-detached house with the main gate and the house itself facing a river flowing from the south-west. To the right of the house is an empty piece of land that's overgrown with lallang, to a height of about five feet.

I get the feeling that the feng shui of my house is out of balance. My children often quarrel and my wife is occasionally unwell. Can you suggest a remedy?

Y.K. Yeap
Ipoh

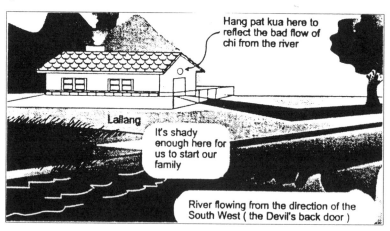

NORMALLY, TALL *LALLANG* facing the house is considered bad feng shui. This is because the tall plant, with its blade-shaped leaves, is said to be 'cutting' the good *chi* flowing towards you. Fortunately, the *lallang* is at the side of your house, so its effect is lessened. In addition to feng shui, tall *lallang* also provides a nesting place for insects, rodents and snakes which may at the very least cause you some inconvenience, or give your family members a scare. Spraying some weed-killer on it would help.

Normally, a river flowing in front of a house is considered good feng shui but in your case, the river flows from the south-west, that is, the Devil's Back Door. This reverses the effect of the river and to counter it, hang a *pakua* over your door.

River and T-junction

THE BACK ROOM of my house faces a stream and a lane which forms part of a T-junction.

What are the implications of this on the occupant of the back room?

Madam Y.K. Lee
Teluk Intan

IT IS NORMALLY deemed lucky to have a stream flowing from behind one's property because it denotes the flowing in of wealth.

But in your case, the lane which forms part of a T-junction has become a negative factor. Wealth is flowing towards the other house which is facing the T-junction.

To control the situation, put an ordinary mirror at a good point in the back room to check the flow of wealth.

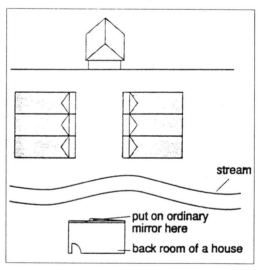

stream

put on ordinary mirror here

back room of a house

Canals

MY HOUSE MAIN door faces the outlet gate of a canal as shown in the diagram. The canal would be flooded when the tide comes in and dries up when the tide goes out.

My main question is, would it be favourable to have the main door of one's house facing the outlet gate? If not, is there any remedy?

G. Subramanian
Pontian

A QUICK LOOK at the diagram tells me that you live in a sort of plantation which is located near the sea. Water represents money in feng shui; so obviously, it is positive sign to have money around one's residence.

But in your situation, having your house entrance facing the outlet gate of the canal which leads to the sea has its pros and cons when it comes to money. When the tide comes in, the canal would be full but when it goes out, so does the water; therefore, your financial situation is like a yo-yo; it keeps going up and down.

There are two possible solutions to this fluctuating state: first, put a huge mirror or reflective object around the doorway to attract the 'water *chi*' back into your house; and second, you could try moving the main door somewhere else, instead of having it face the water outlet gate.

Lakes

WHAT IS THE feng shui of:
- [ ] *A house with a pond in front of it?*
- [ ] *A house facing a lake?*
- [ ] *A house with a lake behind it?*

Mrs P.H. Wong
Kelantan

HAVING A POND or lake facing your house is considered good simply because it means that you are facing lots of money.

Having a lake behind your house means you have already made your money. You must always remember that to have water flowing around your house or its vicinity is better than not having any.

Beach

THE ACCOMPANYING DIAGRAM shows my house, which is facing the sea. We enter the compound through a lane from the back. The front of the house also faces a multi-storey building and its front, a river which runs directly to the sea.

Could you tell me about the feng shui aspect of my house?

J. Yeap
Penang

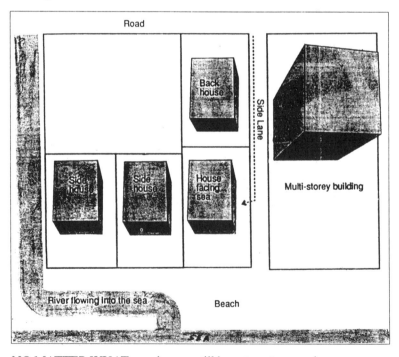

NO MATTER WHAT you do, you still have to enter your house through the side lane as the front faces the beach, and the sides are sandwiched by your neighbour's house and the multi-storey building. The feng shui of your house would be much better if not for the multi-storey building. Having your house facing the sea signifies facing wealth, as the sea has 'limitless' *sui* (water or money).

To have a river running in front of your house towards the sea tells a different story. The occupants of the house may have a lot of money, but finds it hard to hold on to it because of various commitments.

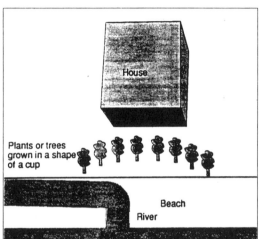

What you can actually do to balance this negative flow is to plant trees in front of your house in a semi-circle. This creates a symbolic cup to get back water which has flowed into the sea.

Water purifier

AFTER I INSTALLED a water purifier in my house, my neighbours (for reasons which I cannot understand as they can easily afford one) have been dropping in to fill their bottles.

If such a practice continues, will it affect the well-being of my family?

Chew Huat Eng
Penang

IN YOUR CASE, one can say that your hospitality has been abused. Habits—either good or bad—just take 30 days to form. And since you have allowed your neighbours to draw water from your house for so long, it will be difficult to tell them to stop.

But what effect does such a practice by your neighbours has on you and your family? If you discount the inconvenience caused by their daily visit, then consider that they take just 10 minutes of your time daily. In simple arithmetic, here is how much time they take from you and your family in a year:

10 minutes x 365 days = 3,650 minutes per year

= 60.66 hours per year or

2.53 days!

If you believe that time is money, then you must believe that your feng shui is being affected. To stop your neighbours from taking further advantage, you have two options:

☐ Tell a salesman of this product that you have neighbours who are fascinated with the water purifier. Invite the salesman to visit your house at the time your neighbours usually come over to fill up their bottles. If the salesman does his job well, he should be able to close an easy sale. However, if he fails to get your neighbours to buy one, and if your neighbours continue to draw water from your house, then try the second option.

☐ Hide your water purifier for a couple of days, and when your neighbours come over, let them know that the frequent usage has exhausted the purifier. They may not believe you initially but if you were to carry on with the deception, they may get frustrated and give up.

Perhaps during this time you can suggest to them that it would be better and easier for them to have a water purifier of their own, than to depend on yours.

PART
9

T-Junctions

T-junction

THERE IS A small lane by the side of my house, and a T-junction in front of the lane.

Does this prevent good chi from coming into my house?

Wee Jeok Kee
Kuantan

A HOUSE MAY or may not face an auspicious direction but it is best if we can avoid facing the junction altogether.

The surge of *chi* coming from the direction of a T-junction is too violent for most occupants.

T-junction and telephone pole

MY HOUSE IS situated in an awkward position. The main entrance into the compound directly faces a T-junction which I understand is bad. Secondly, in a direct line opposite the main door of the house are a telephone pole and a big tree.

If the occupants are out of harmony with the forces of nature, can you offer some advice on how we can overcome the bad chi?

Confused
Penang

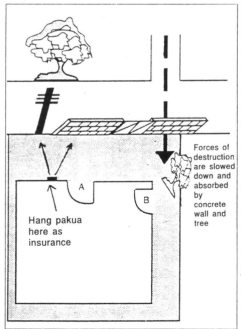

Forces of destruction are slowed down and absorbed by concrete wall and tree

Hang pakua here as insurance

A

B

YOU AND YOUR family are without doubt faced with double-trouble, bombarded by bad forces from both ends. One comes from the T-junction and the other, the phone pole and tree.

What you can do to restore harmony with the natural forces is to shift the main gate so that it is not aligned with the junction. The original site of the gate can be planted with trees to absorb the bad forces emanating from the junction. Alternatively, you can also build an artificial concrete wall at the site to deflect the bad *chi*.

To solve the other problem concerning your main door, you can reduce the impact by chopping down the tree. But that leaves the telephone pole which is a bit tricky to get rid of. So, that leaves you back at square one.

The best solution for you then is to relocate the main door so that it is not in line with the two objects. As shown in the diagram, you have two choices in which to relocate the entrance: slightly to the left or to the side of the house.

Within the range

ENCLOSED IS A PLAN of my house and its surroundings. Could you please read the feng shui of my house?

Feng Shui Follower
Bukit Mertajam

LOOKING AT THE plan of your house, the description does not paint a promising picture. Firstly, part of the house compound falls within the range of the T-junction.

Secondly, an electric pole from the opposite direction faces your main gate, running in line with your main door. As *chi* travels in a straight line, it is considered bad feng shui.

As yours is a terraced house, it is not easy to change the location of your gate or main door. In fact, by shifting

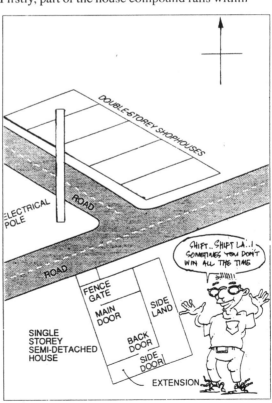

the location of your main door, it may end up nearer the T-junction, which is even worse.

So the best solution is to shift to a new house for better harmony.

White Tiger

MY FAMILY AND I plan to move into a one and a half-storey house which we bought. The house faces west and half our main door partially faces a T-junction. The road in front of our house has 13 houses along it.

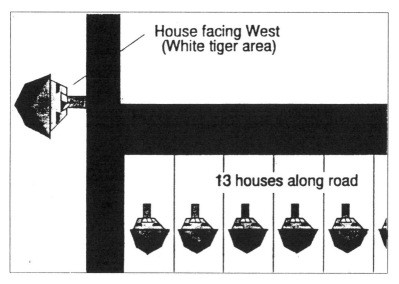

My relatives have advised me to sell the house as they say it is not conducive to 'collecting wealth'. I remember having read in your column that it is all right to stay in such a house as long as a pakua is put up above the door to reflect away the negative elements.

What do you advise?

M.Y. Lee
Kuala Lumpur

IF YOU HAVE a choice between staying in a house which faces a partial T-junction and shifting to a new place, I would advise you to move to a new place. Even though you use a *pakua*, there is still an element of risk. While a *pakua* would help greatly in warding off bad *chi*, there are times when some of these forces are not totally reflected back to their sources.

Taking into consideration your surrounding environment, the signs are not too favourable or in harmony with your house as it faces the west (White Tiger area) with a row of 13 houses which runs along towards your main door.

I only recommend a *pakua* where the owner has no choice but to stay on despite the odds.

Double-storey house at T-junction

MY DOUBLE-STOREY HOUSE stands slightly higher than the row of houses across the road. It faces two buildings with pointed roofs that seem to be aimed at my house. Furthermore, a lane runs between the two. What should I do?

Bad Luck
Kuala Lumpur

HAVING A HOUSE on high ground is always advantageous. In feng shui, however, one should not be confused about the negative forces of sharp points of roofs and the like.

In your case, the roofs of both houses do not have any ill effects for you. As for the lane, your house does not directly face it (as in the case of a T-junction), but its proximity may have some effect on your

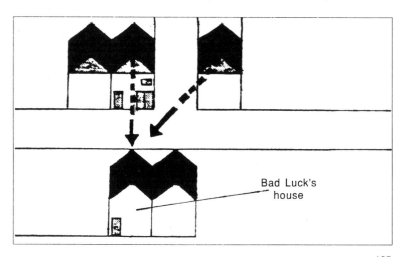

Bad Luck's house

fortune and family life. A tree in your compound could absorb the flow of the undesirable *chi* coming from that direction.

PART
10

Secret Arrows

Neutral and harmful arrows

MY HUSBAND AND I bought a new house which should be ready for occupancy soon. It is a double-storey house with house number 28. It is an intermediate-lot facing the south.

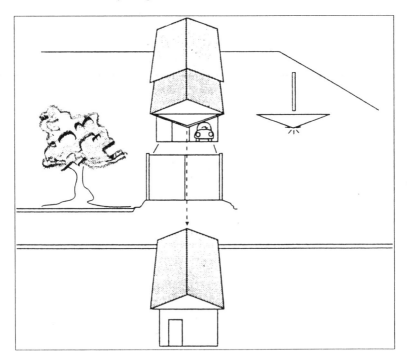

Opposite the house stands a row of semi-detached houses which are currently being built, and I believe they would be ready the same time as my house. Unfortunately, two of the semi-detached units in front of my house have a triangular structure for a porch. We were told

that it is considered bad feng shui to face them. If this is true, how can we rectify the situation?

P.C. Wong
Petaling Jaya

AS MOST ROOFS slope down for the purpose of easy drainage when it rains, some of the corners created by these structures look like arrows. In feng shui, such shapes are called "secret arrows" as they are supposed to bring ill luck to the unfortunate occupants whose houses face them.

But in your case, you have nothing to worry about because those are neutral arrows. They are harmless as the points face upwards. The only time a person should worry is when a roof-top is angled directly towards his direction.

Incidentally, south is a good direction to face, and the number, 28 (*yee fatt*) means "easy to prosper" in Cantonese.

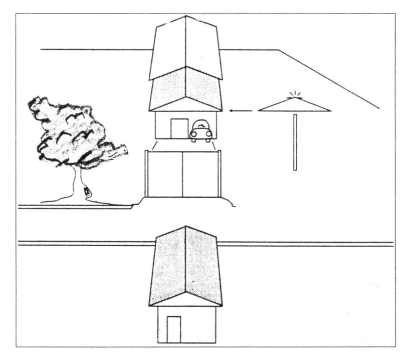

Cutting main gate

MY FATHER HAS a double-storey wooden house which was built in 1940. It sits on a rectangular piece of land, and faces the north. The main gate faces the east. As I have the intention of demolishing this old wooden house and building a modern one, could you please give me some tips on which direction my house and main gate should face?

A.K. Lee
Teluk Intan

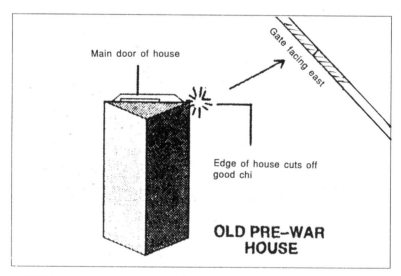

Main door of house

Gate facing east

Edge of house cuts off
good chi

**OLD PRE-WAR
HOUSE**

ALTHOUGH EAST IS a good direction to face, your diagram shows that one of the edges of the house is 'cutting off' the good *chi* coming from that direction. Since you plan to rebuild the house, I would suggest that the gate and the main door face the south-east for a better flow of good luck.

I would like to add that the rectangular plot of land which your house sits on bears a positive element.

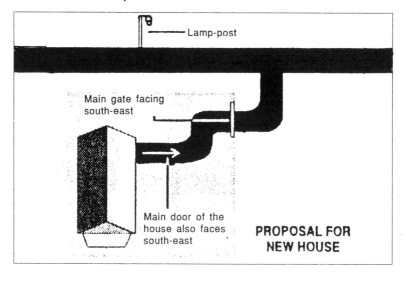

Lamp-post

Main gate facing
south-east

Main door of the
house also faces
south-east

**PROPOSAL FOR
NEW HOUSE**

From edge of house

MY HOUSE FACES the back of a row of other single-unit houses. Besides having an unpleasant view, I have been staying here for 20 years and do not seem to have had much luck. I must say, however, that my health is good. I am now 63.

Occupant
Petaling Jaya

IF YOU TAKE a good look at the diagram you have drawn in illustrating the position of your house, you will notice that your home is being 'cut' by the sharp pointed corner of the house directly opposite.

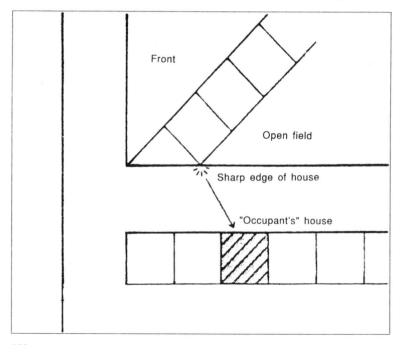

Another point to consider is that your home faces the back of others. As is typical among Asian societies, the kitchen and rubbish dump are located behind the house. Rubbish and dirt pile up here, giving you an unpleasant view and also providing bad feng shui. That is the reason, besides being 'cut' you have not been lucky for the last 20 years.

Put a *pakua* over the main entrance of your house to deflect these bad elements away, and plant a tree to 'blunt' the sharp edge of the house opposite yours.

From school

I AM SENDING you a sketch of two shophouses where I am currently operating a business. The shophouses face due east; opposite is a school-building with one corner and a lamp-post directly across from my place of business. Behind the shop is a lane near which an old tree stands.

I want to know if these factors have put my shop out of harmony and what I can do to enhance the premises' feng shui. Can I counter any bad chi coming from the front of the house by aligning two or three flagpoles and using a mirror to deflect it?

Francis Tan
Ipoh

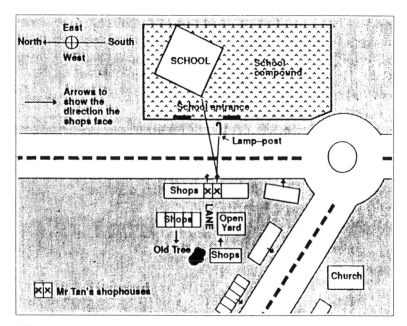

WELL, MR TAN, your shop faces east and that is considered an auspicious direction. But the luck changes because of the school-building's sharp corner 'cutting' into your shop.

This represents a wedge being driven between your business and personal luck and so it is considered to have a negative effect. The lamp-post across the road from your main door is also considered to block the free flow of luck coming in.

The putting up of flagpoles must be given careful thought. If they do not block the entrance of your shop, that is fine. Otherwise, they will just pose as more obstacles to your business.

Putting up a *pakua* at your shop would help balance the forces flowing around the premises.

It is advisable to leave the old tree where it is because it acts like a sort of 'retaining wall' against all your good fortune from flowing off through the lane!

From bedroom

ENCLOSED IS THE layout of my new house. Can you please comment?

Buay Ah Leh
Pontian

WHEN THE ROOM No. 3 door is opened, a 'secret arrow' is formed, shooting *sha chi* towards the direction of Room No. 2. This will cause quarrels and misunderstandings for the occupants of that room.

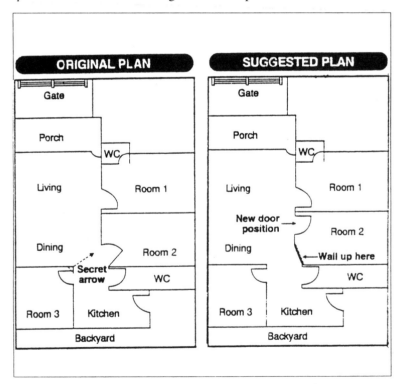

To offset this adverse influence, you can change the door of Room No. 2 to the other side of the wall, and construct a solid wall to close off the old entrance.

As for the secret arrow coming from Room No. 3, place a long bamboo at that sharp angle to control the *sha chi*.

From bedroom wall

I WOULD LIKE to know whether one's sleeping position or a desk placed to face the edge of a wall would affect one's health? And if it does, can you suggest possible remedies that I could take?

L.P. Goh
Kuala Lumpur

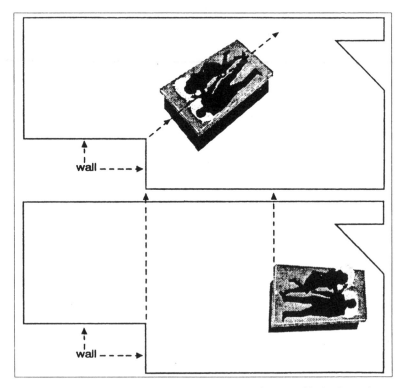

A LOT OF people are under the wrong impression that if a bed or other furniture is placed too near a wall, they are being threatened by a secret arrow. Such belief is wrong because when any furniture is found parallel to a wall, the edge of the wall is not considered that of a secret arrow, thus it has no ill effect on one.

Sharp edges or secret arrows are deemed dangerous, and if one places a table or bed along its path, the edge or the secret arrow will cut into one's direction. Since all secret arrows carry *sha chi*, the effects they cause would all depend on how one places the furniture.

For instance, if one were to sit with an arrow pointing towards his back, physically he may have a spinal problem. Career-wise, he may be backstabbed by his colleagues.

Or if a bed is placed in such a position that a secret arrow cuts it into half, than that would bring bad tidings for the couple and their marriage would most probably break up.

Since most right angles of a wall have hidden *sha chi* to affect us, we can offset their adverse influence by arranging the furniture parallel to the wall.

From cabinet

I HAVE DIFFICULTIES starting a career. As you can see from the illustration, my bedroom furniture touches the wall on the bottom part because of the protruding wall tiles. Does that have anything to do with my situation?

Vyana Foo
Kuala Lumpur

YOUR FOUR-CORNERED CABINET has four secret arrows 'shooting out' from it, and one of them hits you near your head when you go to bed. The other strikes your back when you sit down at the study-table.

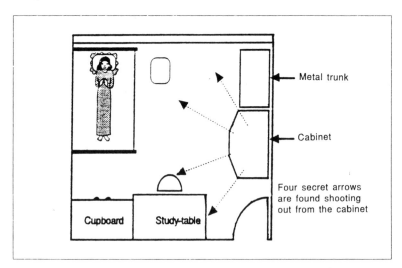

To avoid being 'shot at', I suggest you place your cabinet at one corner of the room as shown. However, there is yet one arrow which may still get you. Block it by sandwiching a four-foot divider between the cabinet and the study-table.

Regarding your bed which does not touch the wall on the upper portion, hammer in two rubber stoppers to bridge the gap. This will give you the support and strength you need.

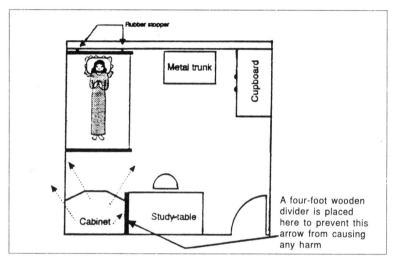

A four-foot wooden divider is placed here to prevent this arrow from causing any harm

From lift

I HAVE BEEN staying at my flat for some time now. However, lately I noticed that a lift nearby has one of its edges pointing towards my unit. Will this affect the feng shui of my unit?

Raymond Tang
Penang

IN YOUR CASE, the flat is found running parallel to your unit, so its sharp edge should not have any ill effect towards you.

Sha chi from TV

MY FAMILY AND I have been renting this apartment for almost four years. I am the sole bread-winner, and I seem to be having financial difficulties. I also miss striking the 4D numbers.

With the salary I am getting, we should be living comfortably and even have some decent savings. But the truth is, we can barely make

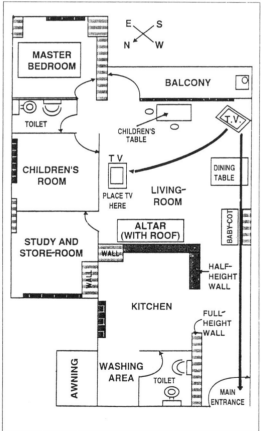

ends meet; money just slips away from our hands. Moreover, my wife and kids fall sick quite frequently.

Is there anything in this apartment that is blocking my luck or is the arrangement of the furniture not right? How can I improve my situation?

Worried Billy Penang

YOUR TV IS placed at such an angle that it is shooting *sha chi* (secret arrows) across your dining-table, baby's cot and main entrance. As the dining-table is a place where food is served, to have it 'cut' by a secret arrow means that one would find hard to make ends meet. Moreover, your main entrance is also affected by the alignment of the secret arrow, so no luck would come your way.

Since the TV is the main culprit here, change its position and place it as indicated in the diagram.

Secret arrows

IF MY BATHROOM has two sharp corners jutting out into the bedroom, will it affect my feng shui?

Feng Shui Believer
Kuala Lumpur

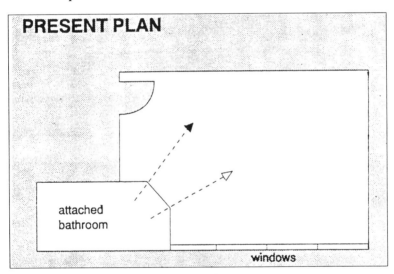

PRESENT PLAN

attached
bathroom

windows

HAVING ONE WALL of the bathrooms slanted, you would note that two secret arrows are formed to shoot its *sha chi*. As a result, the energies tend to 'cut' the room into half.

To create a balance, the best thing to do is to demolish the two arrows by renovating your bathroom into a proper rectangular shape. As energies travel in parallels, you will note that after the renovation, your room will be a more harmonious place to live in. (See the suggested layout below.)

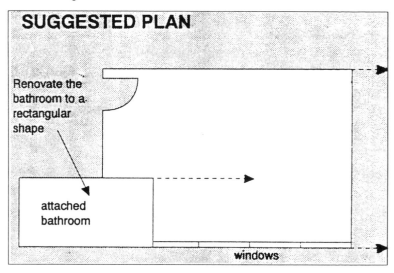

SUGGESTED PLAN

Renovate the bathroom to a rectangular shape

attached bathroom

windows

From personal computer

THERE IS A small mirror inside my bookshelf. Is that likely to send any bad chi in my direction? Please advise how I can improve room's feng shui.

BS
Selangor

YOUR FURNITURE HAS been neatly arranged to ensure harmony in the room. However, there are a couple of things which you should rectify.

It not a good idea to place a mirror in the bookshelf, as it can reflect you image out of the room. So remove, and if you like, you can put it above the table-lamp next to your bed. Next, adjust your PC

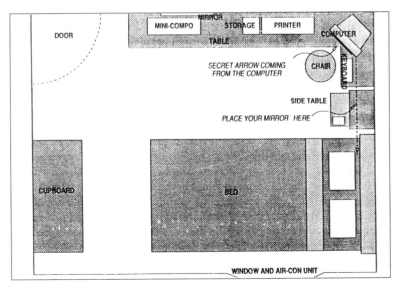

horizontally towards your bed, so that the secret arrow is squared off. As it stands now, your PC is positioned at an angle, and it can be seen as shooting *sha chi* towards your bed.

PART
11

Directions

Compass

CAN YOU PLEASE tell me whether the directions indicated in the Chinese compass and the geographical compass are the same?
When you talk about compass directions, are you referring to the Chinese compass or the geographical compass?

C.G. Tan
Selangor

THERE IS A vast difference between the Geographical compass which points towards the north, and the Chinese *lopan* which points towards the south. Since I have already dealt with the differences in my earlier articles, I will not go into the details again.

When I talk about compass directions, I refer to the geographical compass, unless the *lopan* is specifically mentioned.

Looking for
harmonious direction

ACCORDING TO FENG shui, every person is believed to have a
'harmonious direction' for him to face in order to enjoy good fortune.
Assuming that his direction is south and his house faces north,
what can he do about it if he is unable to move house? Would moving
the bed about or sleeping in a different room suffice?

Lina Lim
Penang

IN DETERMINING THE feng shui of a place, one must not assign its direction or facing sole importance in mapping one's luck. According to priority, the first thing to look out for is the shape of the plot of land. This would tell the geomancer whether or not the house to be built on it would be in the right place.

The second priority is to study the surrounding area: the natural landscape, high-rise buildings or other features have their respective effects on a house. Most of the time, if the shape of the land or the surroundings are found to be unfavourable, a new location can be found before the house is built. Assuming that both the land and its surroundings are in harmony, then changing the location of one's house door is one solution.

North I

I UNDERSTAND THAT it is not auspicious for my house to face north. Is there anything I can do?

Y.P. Ee
Selangor

YOU MAY WANT to relocate your main door. A temporary measure would be to place a *pakua* at the main entrance.

North II

I RECENTLY BOUGHT a house which faces north. My friends had told me that a house which faces north generally has bad feng shui. Is this true?

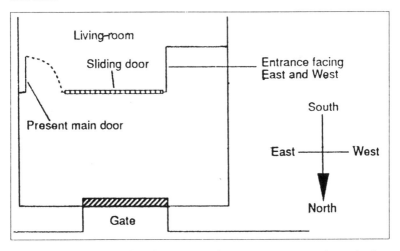

If it is I may consider changing my house entrance (as shown in the diagram). What do you think about this?

JL

GENERALLY SPEAKING, A house facing north is not too good a direction in terms of its feng shui. One way out of your situation is to seal off the front door and relocate it in a more ideal position.

Looking at your plan, it shows that if you were to place a new entrance at the spot marked 'X', you would end up facing west. This is also not considered a very good direction to face in.

If space permits, why not extend your house as shown in the second diagram? In this way, you could have the new door facing east (a good direction) and seal off the current doorway.

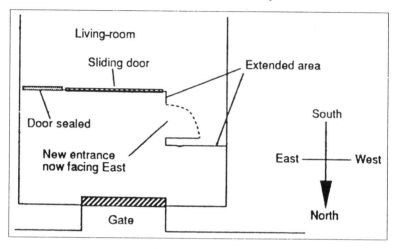

North-east

MY FAMILY MOVED into our double-storey house in 1982. The house faces north-east. I don't consider ourselves to be unlucky, but I would like some advice from you on ways to improve the feng shui and luck.

Wong
Kuala Lumpur

LOOKING AT THE plan you have provided, it can be seen that you have already placed a *pakua* on the front wall of your house as a preventive measure against any bad elements coming in from the north-east.

By placing a *pakua*, you have already neutralized bad *chi* coming from the front. The main entrance to your house faces south-east, which is considered an auspicious direction. So your house is 'in harmony' with its surroundings and likewise, so does your family enjoy harmony.

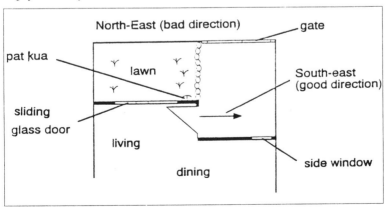

South-west

MY HOUSE, SITUATED in a corner-lot, faces the south-west direction. Directly opposite are houses of a similar design. There is a big shrub full of flowers outside, on the left of the main gate.

I would like to know if it is advisable to leave shoes outside the main door which is in direct line to an altar on which are placed some deities.

Chocolate Honey
Selangor

THE POSITION YOUR house faces is not so auspicious in terms of feng shui. Putting a *pakua* would temporarily restore the balance of bad *chi* emanating from that direction.

The big flowering shrub has not much significance, good or bad, except that it helps to brighten and beautify the surroundings.

Your doubts about placing shoes facing the altar are understand able. It is not ideal to place footwear directly in front of places of worship.

In the olden days, commoners used to prostrate in the presence of royalty and personages of power as a show of respect and reverence. As feet are the lowest parts of the body, shoes and other accessories worn or used to cover them should not be placed facing an altar. Doing so is an act of utter disrespect. Since most of us remove our shoes before entering the house, footwear could be placed at one corner of the house, away from the entrance instead of in front of the altar or place of worship.

The Devil's
Back Door

MY HOUSE FACES south-west and has its gate and front door grille painted black. The front door is made of wood, which is brown in colour. Could you tell me which colour I should use if I want to repaint them?

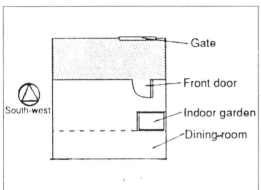

I also have an indoor garden which is planted mostly with ferns. I hear that such a garden should have a pond or fountain to represent wealth.

As my indoor garden is in line with the front door and front gate of the house, is there any adverse effect caused by such positioning?

Mrs Teh
Petaling Jaya

AS MENTIONED EARLIER, Mrs Teh, the south-west direction is known as the Devil's Back Door. I suggest that if you have some money to spare, you may want to consider doing some extension work to the front of your house. If you can, position your door facing south-east. Or else, repaint your black gate white and place a *pakua* over the door to disperse the bad *chi*.

You need not worry about the garden because there is a concrete wall after the front door to prevent *chi* from flowing in a straight line. Having green plants in an indoor garden is a positive

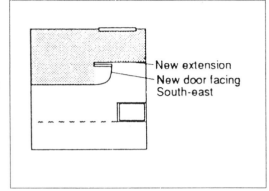

New extension
New door facing South-east

thing because plants give off oxygen and good *chi* that would definitely benefit the occupants of the house.

Whether or not it is good to have a fountain or waterfall in an indoor garden to represent wealth and good feng shui depends on where exactly you put them.

West

THE PLACE MY family and I live in was formerly a storehouse which has been converted and partitioned into a house. It belongs to my grandfather.

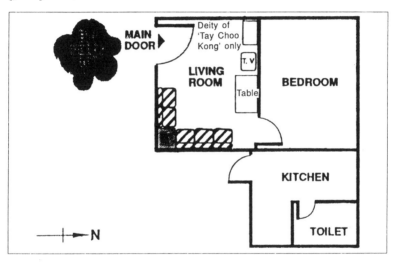

The main 'door' of the dwelling faces about 6 degrees west from the true south direction. I have fixed a mirror above the main door because of a big mango tree which is directly in front of the entrance.

At the moment, my wife, children and myself live in the house. Financially, we have made no progress at all. Health-wise, the children are always falling sick.

Your advice will be greatly appreciated.

S.T.
Penang

Practical Feng Shui for the Home

FROM THE PLAN you submitted, your built-up area is rather small and I don't think it will be practical to shift the positions of your furniture to get the best out of the feng shui.

The fact that your entrance faces south is quite good. But because of the obstacle—the big mango tree which lies in the path of any good *chi* flowing towards your house—progress or success is impeded.

My recommendation would be to shift the entrance so that it faces the east.

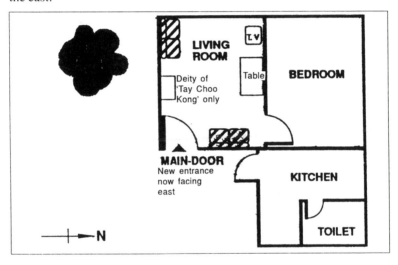

Share market tip

I SHALL BE retiring at the end of the year and moving back to my hometown. I have two corner- lot houses which are rented out at the moment. One faces the north, the other the north-west.
I am a small investor in the share market and hope to make some extra cash. I hope you can advise me on where to live in order to receive more luck.

Madam LSP
Shah Alam

THE NORTH IS a cold place where life is almost absent. It is a fitting direction for the home of a pensioner to face. However, since you do not intend to retire fully but to remain active in the share market, you should choose the other house.

In China, water flows from the west into the interiors. So money will still flow to you if you live in a house which faces the north-west.

To get something positive out of the stock market, don't be greedy. Invest only if you can afford to. Otherwise, you may lose all your pension money.

Part
12

Frontings

The pole

I LIVE IN a single-storey house which faces a double-storey house. A pole bearing electrical cables is opposite my house, to our left. My mother-in-law placed a pakua over the door before we moved in.

Does the presence of pole cause bad feng shui even though it is not directly in front of my house?

Lim Lee Peng
Petaling Jaya

SUCH POLES ARE found everywhere these days; if you want to be free of them, you would have to live in the jungle where there is no electricity supply and there is only darkness for companion.

If a house faces a good direction, and an object is in front of it, then in feng shui we consider it unlucky since our luck is being blocked. In your case, as the pole is not directly in front of your house, there are no ill effects.

The *pakua* may be left in place; it does not have any adverse effect on you and your family.

Street-light

MISS GOH SEE Meng of Kuala Lumpur asks on a friend's behalf if a street-light directly in front of the main door means the house has bad feng shui. Her friend says that when the street-light is turned on at night, it gives the impression of a mortuary where a light is left on throughout the night.

"If the above is true," Miss Goh writes, "could you advise us on any improvements? Otherwise, my friend may consider moving to a safer area."

Sometimes, problems in the understanding of feng shui can arise when certain essential details are not furnished. In these cases, an overactive imagination and superstition can lead one to undesirable conclusions.

There are so many street-lights around today that comparing one to a mortuary light is somewhat far-fetched. About the only effect of street-lights on feng shui is when a lamp-post is directly in front of your house.

In purely physical terms, the street-light outside the house would merely cause a distraction to those inside who are trying to sleep, especially if the light shines through the bedroom windows.

No-entry signs

THE MAIN DOOR of my house faces a T-junction and two no-entry signs. The land that my house is situated on is slightly higher than the main road. There is also a hill behind the road.

To have some privacy, I have planted some shrubs along the fence. Please advise me on the feng shui of this situation.

Edward Lam
Miri

A HILL AT the back of one's house always carries a positive element in feng shui as it shields your back and at the same time, gives you added strength to turn back whatever unwanted elements approach from the front. Another positive point is that your house, too, is on high ground.

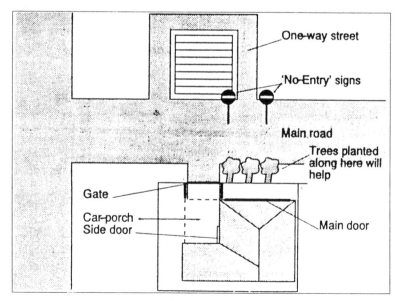

Your house faces the notorious T-junction and a *pakua* will help to cancel out its effect.

The no-entry signs, however, are a stumbling block to your progress. A *pakua* may help but ultimately there is little else you can do as the signs are not on your property.

Both ways

*I UNDERSTAND THAT a pole or lamp-post in the front of main door of
one's house is considered bad feng shui. Can you clarify this?*

S.L. Yeo
Kuala Lumpur

THERE IS A story that can answer your question, albeit a long one.
Every now and then, we hear stories of how some folks from the small
town manage to make it big in the city. City life can be cruel to those
who attempt to fit in there, and often the price to pay for coming to the
city is a loss of innocence. Those who fight hard may find rewards;
they are the fittest, who have survived.

One such person—let's call her Jane—decided that there were
dreams she could realize in the big city. Having found a job as a
secretary in a good firm, she rented a small terraced house together
with some friends. Jane was a sociable girl, and found it easy to get
along with almost everyone. In the evenings, she took up management
classes in the belief that it would give her an edge over her colleagues
when the 'right time' came along.

One day, an acquaintance suggested that a tree growing outside the
house and facing the front door could mean bad luck. The acquaintance
continued by telling Jane that her boss, who also had a tree growing in
front of his house, consulted a mysterious man who 'knew the ways of
nature'. The man advised her boss to cut down the tree, which he did.

Within the next couple of weeks, she said, her boss' luck changed
for the better and his business picked up. This played on her mind until

she got home, when she called a woodcutter. After the usual haggling, they agreed on the fee and she arranged to have the tree cut.

Finally, the tree was felled and Jane felt her luck would change. For the next couple of weeks, she forgot the whole episode. Her career and life moved into the fast lane. Her boss informed her that a management position had become vacant and promoted her. Furthermore, the company was expanding and her management training came in useful in getting her the job.

Then Jane bought a lottery ticket, her only intention being to help the invalid who was selling it. The ticket was the first one she had ever bought.

One day, as she was casually flipping through the pages of a newspaper, the lottery results caught her eye. She took the solitary lottery out of her purse and could not believe her eyes: she had won the first prize!

After a week or two, Jane decided she no longer needed the rented room. She bought and moved into a new house. She also bought a new sportscar and went into business on her own. However, business is never an easy thing to venture into, especially for someone who is 'green'. Anyway, believing she benefit from the beginner's luck she went ahead.

She set up her own business with the money left over from her lottery winnings. A few months later, however, the returns from her business had turned out to be less than what she expected. Many businessmen and managers would be quick to tell you that any new business would take time to bear fruit. Jane had not considered this.

One evening, as a tired Jane drove home, she saw the tree growing across the road from her new house and remembered her friend's story. Could this tree be preventing her from making a success of the business?

. . . history does not always repeat itself.

She ran inside her house and called the woodcutter again. The grumpy man refused to come over, until Jane said she would pay him $200 to cut down the tree.

Realizing she was desperate, he bargained up to $300 and agreed to come over immediately. Soon, he had arrived and was hard at work. At last the tree fell with a noisy crash.

Jane thought to herself: "It is so easy. You see a tree in front of your house, you just cut it down and you're on the road to success."

However, history does not always repeat itself. For the next couple of months things got worse. Jane eventually had to wind up her company as her creditors sued her for bankruptcy.

A feng shui expert who did a study of this incident found out that the first house Jane had rented had a good feng shui which was being blocked by the tree. So, once that tree had been felled, the good feng shui began to flow in.

The second house, however, faced a bad direction in terms of feng shui and it was only the tree that was acting as a shield to ward off some of the negative flow. Once Jane had that tree cut down, the floodgates for bad *chi* were opened.

This story shows that a tree or pole can have a good or a bad effect, depending on the conditions. Most importantly, it tells you to be thoroughly aware of a situation before taking any action.

Lifeless symbol

WE HAVE JUST shifted to our apartment which is on the first floor. There is a big dead tree just outside our main window. To avoid any problems, we placed a pakua on our altar which faces the direction of the tree.

Is there any other way I can prevent any negative chi from affecting my family?

May Cheong
Shah Alam

A DEAD TREE highlighted by the street-lights at night can be a grotesque sight. Besides, a dead tree is a symbol of lifelessness.

The best thing for you to do would be to cut down this dead tree which carries bad *chi*. This would give your family a clearer view from the window and bring about better harmony with the environment.

Withered tree

ENCLOSED IS A plan of my house and its surroundings. Can you please comment on the feng shui?

Worried
Shah Alam

AS THE HOUSE opposite yours is situated on higher ground, it will enjoy better feng shui than your house. I note too, that your house faces the north-east, which is known as the Devil's Direction. You can relocate the front gate to face north as shown in the diagram below, to create better harmony.

There is a withered tree in front of your house, which symbolizes emptiness and fruitlessness. Perhaps you could chop it down, so that you can make more progress in your career.

Northern tree

MADAM JEE OF Selangor writes that her house, which faces north, has its gate and main grille door painted black. A large tree is located directly opposite the gate and door of her house. She wants to know how she may offset the bad feng shui caused by all this.

Well, Madam Jee, having your gate and main door painted black is not a good idea considering where they are facing. So you may have some repainting to do in the near future. Any colour apart from black will do fine.

In feng shui, north is not considered a good direction for a house to be facing. In fact, you are very lucky to have that huge tree in front of it. The tree actually protects the occupants of the house by blocking and absorbing all the bad *chi*

Lucky you have this tree here, otherwise.. .. bad pung shui!

that is flowing from the north. And for that, you should be thankful.

Tree stump

THE HOUSE I am living in is number nine and it faces a field. Near the gate, there is a shrine. In the front garden, an old, four-foot tree stump lies just opposite the main entrance of the house.

Shall I place a pakua at my main entrance or should I just remove the stump?

Mr Chan
Petaling Jaya

THE NUMBER NINE or *cheong kow* literally carries the meaning "long life". It can also mean "everlasting" or "forever".

But to have a four-foot dead tree stump facing your main entrance is bad feng shui because a dead stump reflects no life. It also measures four feet (*sei* means death), so there is a double negative here. If it is left at your door step, all your ventures will be unsuccessful.

The shrine which is placed near the main gate of your house can do little to protect you as the stump stands in its way, thus blocking its effectiveness.

Placing a *pakua* at the main entrance will help to ease the problem but the best solution is to remove the stump.

Mango tree and lamp-post

*NOT LONG AFTER moving into my new house, my working
relationship with my boss has gone 'off' somehow.*

*My luck has not been too good either. I think it could be caused by
the lamp-post and mango tree directly opposite my house. What do you
think?*

**Raymond Chow
Ipoh**

WELL, RAYMOND, MOVING into a house with a mango tree in
front of it could cause your relationship with your boss to turn sour.

Your luck changing for the worse can be attributed to the street-
light which shines at night on the tree, highlighting its negative effect.

You could cut down the tree to reduce the negative influence of
your surroundings. However, the street-light is still a force to reckoned
with, and it is not likely that you can get it removed.

Therefore, the best thing for you to do is move to a new home for a
change of luck, rather than lock horns with what you cannot beat.

Faces toilet

I HAVE SHIFTED into a double-storey house in which the landlord has renovated the toilet.

The problem is that whenever we have our main door open, we find ourselves facing the toilet in our neighbour's house.

Ganes V.
Selangor

SINCE THE HOUSE you are staying in is a rented one, it is best that you do not do any major renovation.

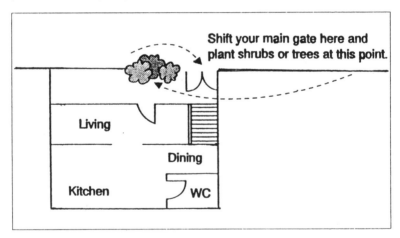

However, to have your main entrance facing somebody's toilet is not too positive for feng shui since it is an area where waste is deposited. What you can do is to move your main gate to one side of the house as illustrated in the diagram. As for the former gate area, plant a tree or two to block the toilet from being seen from your main door.

Sewers

THERE IS A sewage tank right behind my house. I am an assistant manager and my career is stagnant. A number of joint ventures with my brother-in-law have ended up being abandoned. Does the sewage tank have anything to do with this?

Lim Kok Tong
Kuala Lumpur

IN FENG SHUI, to have a hill or a mountain directly behind one's home is to have a solid back-up in life. However, a sewage tank symbolizes waste and to have it as a back up means that your endeavours are doomed from the start.

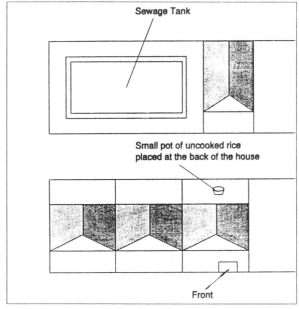

The best solution is to move house. If not, fill up a small pot with uncooked rice and place it at the back of your house to promote a new growth of luck.

Sewage pond

MY HOUSE IS located near a sewage pond. The pond gives off a horrible smell when the wind blows towards my house. This is a newly developed housing area and I have been staying here for nine months. Is there any solution to my problem?

M. Theresa
Klang

EACH DAY YOU are at the mercy of the wind. When it blows towards your house, because of the sewage pond, you will definitely have an unpleasant experience.

It is considered bad feng shui to live in such an area. The sewage is also infested with bacteria. Staying near a sewage pond and breathing in its foul odour will not affect you immediately, but in the long run it may not be too healthy.

It is not easy to wake up in the early morning and be greeted by a foul smell. Nor is it nice to come home to it after a hard day's work. You can further imagine how difficult it would be having dinner, watching television or trying to get a good night's sleep.

Right before buying a house, you should check out the surrounding area by asking the developer to show you around, or going there yourself. Once a buyer signs a sale and purchase agreement without looking at the site of his house, he is taking a great risk. The nightmare will start when he moves in, or finally gets to view the house, only to find something undesirable, like a sewage pond,

facing it. He can make as much noise as he wants, but little can be done then. As the ancient saying goes, *caveat emptor* (let the buyer beware).

The are only two options you can choose from:

☐ Plant some trees in front of the sewage pond to absorb some of the smell.

☐ The best solution is to move away.

Dead trees and
sewage ponds

MY HOUSE SITS on higher ground facing the south. There's a strip of land in front—with dead trees—which awaits replanting. A small river flows alongside my house. Now and then, there's an obnoxious smell in the air as my house is also near an oil palm sewage pond.
Is it advisable to stay on or should I move somewhere else?

Liew Kew Chai
Kamunting

WHILE IT IS good that your house is on higher ground and faces the south, other factors could undermine the positive feng shui.

Firstly, the dead trees in front of your house signify zero growth in life, even though there's a river flowing parallel to your dwelling. A quick replanting would definitely

River

Hilly area

Land awaiting replanting

SEWAGE

Evil chi from nearby sewage pond

help. Then there's the obnoxious smell around, which is not within your control. This may not be healthy for you and your family. So if you can, move out and look for a more conducive environment elsewhere.

Rubbish dump

MY HOUSE WHICH is a corner-lot faces a row of badly maintained squatter homes. They have no proper drainage, sewage or garbage removal, and this stinks up the neighbourhood.

Moreover, there is a rubbish dump, obviously created by the squatters next to my house. Ever since I bought the house and moved in last year, I have faced many problems and am always depressed.

Nothing seems to be working right for me. So please advise me on the remedial action I can take.

Problems Galore
Kuala Lumpur

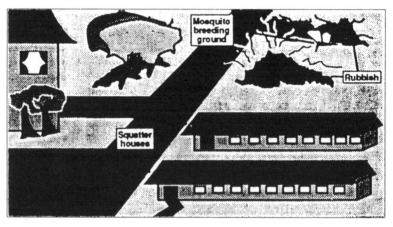

YOUR HOUSE FACES east which is good, but the adjacent rubbish dump created by the squatters changes all that. The poor drainage and sewage removal result in unhygienic conditions around your area, especially in providing a very conducive breeding ground for mosquitoes.

The foul smell would also have an unhealthy influence on you and the other occupants of your house. Your body would definitely be unset by the stench every time you are at home. Thus, when you cannot find peace at home, you will be depressed and find it hard carrying out your daily affairs.

What you need to do is make an official complaint to the authorities to clean up the place; or you could ask your neighbours to join you in a *gotong-royong* campaign.

You could also buy some air ionizers and place them at various strategic locations around your house, to purify the atmosphere. This would have a positive effect on your mental and physical well-being.

There is little else to do in this matter; you cannot compromise on your health.

Gun

I AM A detective, and have a room in a police station which faces east. It is built on higher ground than the playground opposite. The problem is, there are two new see-saws at the playground, pointing towards my direction. The nearest see-saw is 12 meters from my office. From where I sit, I can see it through the glass window, and it seems to be pointing towards the left side of my head. I feel very uneasy about this.

I would like to know if this has any adverse effects, and if so, is there any remedial action I can take? Please don't ask me to put up a mirror or pakua at the main entrance as it is not my property. If planting a tree or two would help, then I can consider it.

T.C. Lim
Pahang

FROM THE POINT of feng shui, it is a positive thing to have one's office on higher ground. East is a good direction to face, too. But in your profession the see-saw, which bears the symbol of a gun, could become a threat or hindrance as it is pointing towards your head.

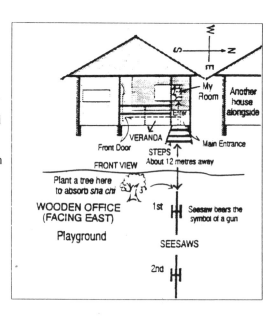

Yours is a high-risk job as you are in the security forces and your life could be at stake. Since it is not convenient for you to put up a *pakua*, perhaps you can write to the proper authority and suggest that the see-saw be placed elsewhere in the playground.

If that is not possible, then perhaps you can plant a tree to absorb the deadly *sha chi*. But make sure that the tree is kept under control because if it becomes too big, it can work to your disadvantage as it will block your view of the front.

Ice

CHEAH CHENG YU of Klang is renting a shoplot with a public road and a private car-park behind it. At the front of the shop, an ice-seller has stacked up block upon block of ice.

Mr Cheah says he cannot ask the ice-seller to move because it is a public area. He wishes to know if this poses any hindrance to the feng shui of his shop.

Well, in many cases, a car-park directly behind your shop could mean that your business and fortune could come to a standstill. Furthermore, having blocks of ice facing your shop could mean that the progress of your good fortune has been frozen solid.

When you notice that your business is not moving in any positive direction, it would mean that your situation—being sandwiched by these two influences—has made your current location an undesirable place for your trade.

Manhole

THE FRONT DOOR of my house faces a manhole and a backlane
formed by two rows of terrace houses with their backs to each other. In
the distance is a small hill.
        Can I do anything to improve the feng shui of my house?

Lam Kam Choong
Kuala Lumpur

TO HAVE A house facing a hill is considered bad luck as the hill
symbolizes a blockage to one's progress in life. Your problem is further
compounded by the fact that your house faces a backlane where
rubbish is disposed of. The manhole in front of your gate symbolizes
fortune being siphoned away.

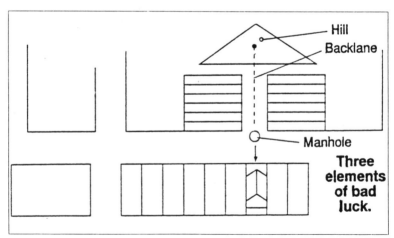

Three elements of bad luck.

Putting a *pakua* in front of your house might help to reflect some of
the bad luck away. But as there are so many adverse factors affecting

your dwelling, it would be best for you to move away and find another place which enjoys better harmony with nature.

Swing

KELVIN KOH OF Kuala Lumpur has his house facing an open
playground. He has planted a coconut tree and two papaya trees just
outside the house and to the right.

He is seeking advice on the feng shui of the house.

Well, firstly, your house faces the sunrise, which is a good
direction. However, having the four swings of the playground in front
of your house does have its negative aspects.

This is because whenever a swing is in use, its motion represents a
tiger opening its mouth. It is said that to face a tiger's mouth in such a
manner is to experience poor health and bad luck.

Your plan shows that only one of the four swings is right in front of
your house; this is fortunate, or you would have four 'tigers' across the
road.

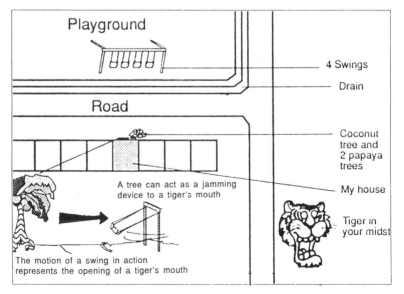

Playground

4 Swings

Drain

Road

Coconut
tree and
2 papaya
trees

A tree can act as a jamming
device to a tiger's mouth

My house

Tiger in
your midst

The motion of a swing in action
represents the opening of a tiger's mouth

So what can you do about it? Well the trees you planted would thwart the 'swallowing' movements of the tiger's mouth. Using this remedy, you still have to regularly tend the trees you have planted. As an extra precaution, you may want to place a *pakua* over the entrance of your house.

Playground I

I LIVE IN a double-storey corner-house which faces south. The doors and window grilles are black, while the gate is grey-brown in colour. The house also faces a playground which is on a higher level (by about 1.5 meters or five feet). I want to know what kind of feng shui the house has in store for my family and I.

Susan Lee
Kuala Lumpur

WELL, SUSAN, A house facing south is not considered bad. However, the field across the road, which is 1.5 meters higher, poses a setback to your feng shui because it 'overshadows' your house.

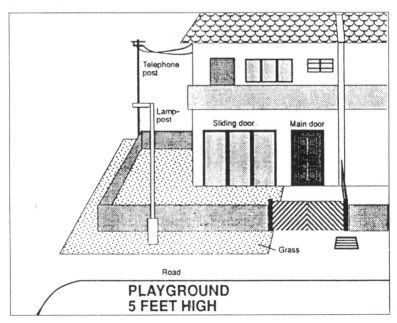

If your house had been a single-storey one, the occupants' progress would have come to a standstill because the field acts as a symbolic mountain, thus creating a kind oɪ blockage. But since your house is a double-storey building it is not completely overshadowed.

The grilles and doors should be painted in a more neutral colour, such as white or yellow, as it is considered bad for the colour black to clash with a cardinal direction like north and south.

Furthermore, when combined with the playground in front of your house this would definitely cast some 'dark shadows' over your house front.

As the field cannot be moved away, try placing a *pakua* over your door.

Playground II

THREE YEARS AGO I shifted into my present house. It faces a football pitch which is five meters deep. Does this have any adverse implications on the feng shui of my house?

Madam Boey

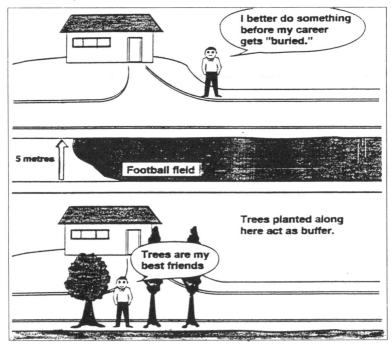

A BIG HOLE or deep pitch in front of one's house could spell different implications for different individuals. If you were a businesswoman it could mean that your business would be buried inside the hole, or in other words, stagnate. If you were a career woman, this could be a hindrance as far as promotion is concerned.

To curb the ill effects, you should plant some trees opposite your house. This would act as a buffer between you and the pitch.

Wall

I MOVED INTO my new house a few months ago and have since been retrenched by my employer. I still could not find any logical explanation for losing my job.

However, I did notice that the people who worked with seemed to be turning against me in my final months on the job.

After having read all your articles, I realize that the corner-house across the road has a wall that runs perpendicular to my main entrance. Could this wall be harming my home's chi? If so, is there a way to overcome it?

Puzzled

WELL, PUZZLED, I really wonder whether you noticed that the paper you wrote to me on has the number 14 on it.

Probably, since your mind was preoccupied with other worries, you did not notice it and used the sheet of paper without realizing its

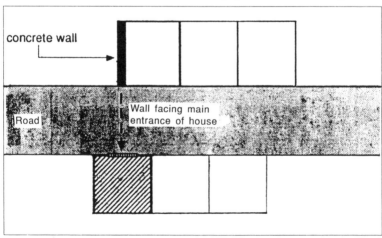

significance. You have noticed that your main door faces a long wall from across the road. You also believe that this has some negative bearing on your luck. Well, for an "amateur geomancer", you are absolutely right.

A man-made wall running perpendicular to the main entrance of your home does create an obstacle and causes an imbalance of *chi*. As a result, your progress of late has been blocked.

Since the wall is not your property, you cannot demolish it. So the best thing for you to do is to place a *pakua* over your main door to ward off the negative effects of the wall. I believe that if you do so, your luck should change for the better.

MY HOUSE FACES east, and there is a hill about 10 meters ahead. To the left is a lamp-post. Around the back, there is a telephone pole right in the middle. The front gate main entrance and kitchen door are aligned.

Sze Mei
Selangor

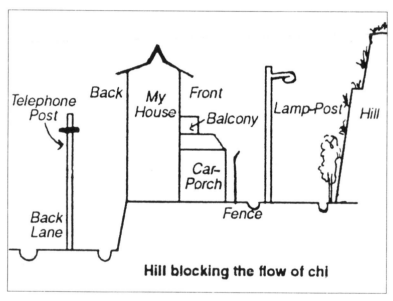

Hill blocking the flow of chi

A HOUSE FACING east is good, but when a hill looms up close as in your situation then the good *chi* coming from that direction will certainly be blocked. When the 'mouth' of the house is closed in this way, then the tenants will certainly not derive any benefit.

What you can do immediately is move the main entrance of your house to one side so that all your main doors are not aligned. Such alignment causes whatever little *chi* there is to flow out easily.

Putting up a *pakua* would be fine if you only needed to deflect undesirable minor forces, but when it comes to a hill, it is like a man wearing a bulletproof vest trying to stop a cannonball.

For best results, of course, you could look for a new home where the feng shui is better or stay, if there are plans for the hill to make way for development.

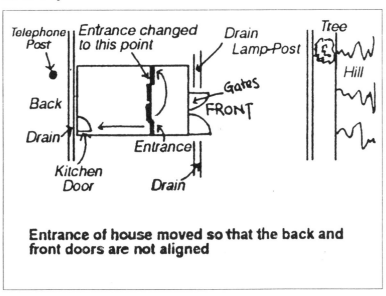

Entrance of house moved so that the back and front doors are not aligned

Artificial mountain

CAN AN 'ARTIFICIAL mountain' block one's path in life? I have been living in my present house for 28 years, since birth as a matter of fact. To date, the family fortunes have remained stagnant. Whatever we earn would be just enough to last us till the end of the month, with nothing left to spare.

Our house number is 20B and a hydrant is found on the left outside the house. From the opposite direction, house No. 19 is built on higher ground. House 20A, which is on a smaller piece of land, adjoins our house on the left.

Rajah
Penang

THE HYDRANT ON the far left does not hold much significance for the feng shui of your house. The real culprit is right in front of you: house No. 19 which stands on higher ground.

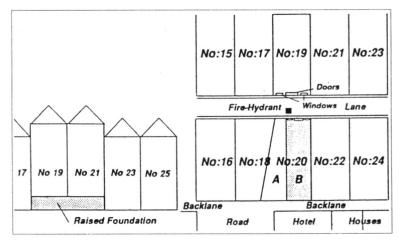

In feng shui, we say that an 'artificial mountain' has blocked your path and when you are faced with such an obstruction, your destiny and progress in life are also held up.

There are two things you could do: to literally smash your way through a mountain—especially this one—would not be possible, since other people live in it. So you could move house or, if circumstances do not permit this, put up a *pakua* to correct the imbalance.

Temple I

K.K. NG OF Penang has a problem with his house, which he has put up for sale. He has brought a number of prospective buyers to view the place, but after the usual guided tour, each one has commented that the house is facing a temple.

Therefore, he says the potential buyers all backed down because they felt that this situation would bring bad feng shui for the occupants of the house.

Well, Mr Ng, many of those who believe in the practice of feng shui would prefer not to live too close to a place of worship, or to have their homes facing such places.

In my opinion, many people go to places of worship out of some obligation. Sometimes, they have a boon to ask, some personal problems to solve. The vibrations, of *chi*, that emanates from a place where people come to seek help with their many problems, are often strong and unpredictable. So it is best for people not to live too close to such areas.

Vortex of energy coming from the temple

If you are looking for a prospective buyer, the best type would be a devotee who regularly visits this particular temple in front of your house. He may like the idea because the proximity of his residence and place of worship would save a lot on travelling time and expenses. And being a devotee at that temple, he would probably not be mindful of any unpredictable consequences of living close to it.

Temple II

ENCLOSED IS A plan of my house and its surroundings. Can you please tell me what are the factors which contribute to disharmony among the occupants?

Unhappy
Kedah

MOST RELIGIOUS PLACES exert a unique spiritual influence and they are normally guarded by some special shield against hostile influences.

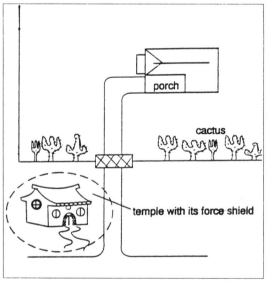

This shield which protects the temple may have an adverse effect on houses nearby. Besides that, a temple also absorbs all positive energy from its surroundings and houses nearby would eventually lose their vitality and good feng shui. And if the temple prospers, the wealth can be said to have come from its neighbours. Thus it is best to avoid living too near a temple.

If for some reason or other, you are unable to move house, then plant some cacti or other thorny plants in front of your house to protect its feng shui.

Used temple

MY DOUBLE-STOREY TERRACED house faces the east and is on higher ground than the row of houses opposite.

Since moving in three years ago, luck and good health seem to evade us. Could it be due to:

☐ *The trees in my compound?*

☐ *The cross-road?*

☐ *The drain around my house, as it is an end-lot?*

☐ *The house opposite which was used as a temple for a year?*

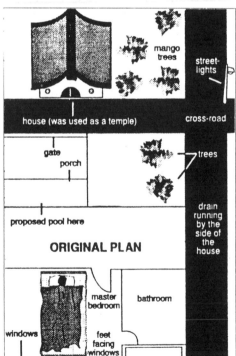

mango trees

street-lights

house (was used as a temple)

cross-road

gate

porch

trees

drain running by the side of the house

proposed pool here

ORIGINAL PLAN

master bedroom

bathroom

windows

feet facing windows

I plan to place a children's play-pool where the present car-porch stands. Is that all right?

Our master bedroom is located at the back of the house. The position of the bed is such that our feet end up facing the windows when we sleep. Is there any adverse implication in feng shui?

Curious
Kuala Lumpur

THE TREES,
CROSS-ROAD and drain

found outside your house have no adverse effects on the feng shui of the place, but the same cannot be said of the house opposite which was used as a temple.

Water can act as a neutralizing agent. Since you plan to place a children's pool outside your house, you might as well put it in a more strategic location to offset the negative influences coming from the opposite direction.

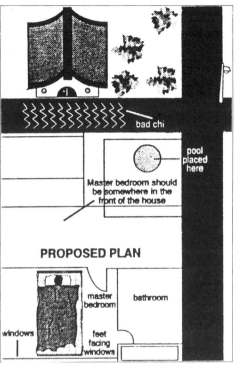

bad chi

pool placed here

Master bedroom should be somewhere in the front of the house

PROPOSED PLAN

master bedroom

bathroom

windows

feet facing windows

As head of the household, your master bedroom should be in the front portion of the house and not the back. There is no harm in sleeping with your legs towards the window.

Higher road

I STAY IN a house where the road outside is higher than the house. Every morning, I have to drive my car up a slope to reach the main road outside.

I have heard that it is not good to live in such an environment. Is this true? Is there any way of overcoming this?

CSC
Kuala Lumpur

IN NORMAL CIRCUMSTANCES, it is not good to live in a house that has a road outside that is on higher ground. The practical reasons include:

☐ *Health*. You must remember that living in such a house is considered bad feng shui. A main road is like having a gas pipeline running by your house because of vehicles constantly moving along it. Pollutants from these vehicles will be harmful to the occupants health in the long run.

☐ *Accidents*. There is a possibility that vehicles may skid off the road and onto the house. There is a no way to predict when or if this would happen.

☐ *The mysterious chi*. The flow of *chi* along the road will 'cut' through your house like a knife, bringing disharmony.

☐ *Peeping Toms*. You never know when the curious, the busybody, or the pervert might decide to peep into your house from the road above.

☐ *Flood*. As water finds its own level, there is always a danger living on lower ground because heavy rainfall may lead to flooding.

☐ *Landslide*. There is always the possibility of this happening if the soil on the slope is not held in check by a barrier or retaining wall.

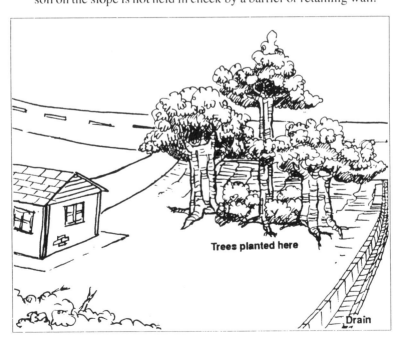

Trees planted here

Drain

What you can do to cope:

☐ *Plant trees.* Trees are beneficial if you know how to use them. To a certain extent, the foliage helps to filter the foul air. Trees can also form a type of shield against noise and vehicles in case they skid off the road and head in the direction of your house. They also help to break up the 'blade' of *chi* that may cut through your house, and provide shade and a screen to keep prying eyes out.

☐ *Change the entrance.* If possible, create another entrance to the house, preferably in the opposite direction. This way, you will have reversed your front entrance and put the higher road at the back of your house.

Cobra

ON THE LEFT of my house is a mountain range with a head shaped like a cobra. From the illustration, can you tell if my house is sited in an auspicious area?

Mrs Wong
Ipoh

THE MOUNTAIN WITH a cobra head does not face your house, so you need not worry. As your house is sited near the tail of the snake, you will find that you have much control of most situations in life.

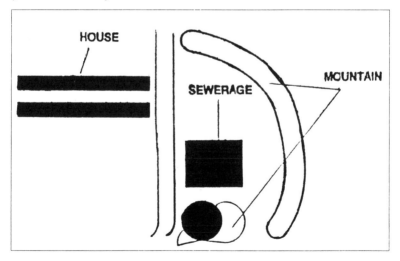

Army camp

MY HOUSE IS an intermediate double-storey split-level terrace which faces the south-east with a reservoir on the top of a hill.

At the back of the house is another hill where an army camp is based. Sometimes, live ammunition is fired in their firing range. The sound that echoes from there is a nuisance.

H.K. Lim
Penang

THE RESERVOIR REPRESENTS the elements of water in feng shui while the army camp represents fire due to its aggressive nature.

In theory, the element of water would subdue the element of fire. However, as your place of stay lies in the space between the two forces, there is a struggle between the elements. The environment thus is not in your favour.

If you are looking for progress in your career, the best thing to do is look for a more receptive place to live in.

Cemetery

ENCLOSED IS A sketch of my house and its surroundings. Please comment on its feng shui.

C.K. Wah
Taiping

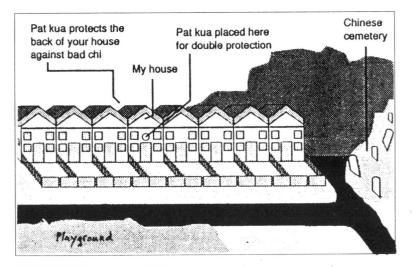

TO LIVE IN a house just 150 meters away from a cemetery is considered too close for comfort as it is believed that the living and the dead should not be residing together. It is even worse if the house faces the cemetery. But in your case, since the cemetery is located at the side with four lots to block off the bad *chi*, the adverse effect is thus reduced.

I note from your diagram that you have placed a *pakua* at the back of your house. To be on the safe side, you should also place a *pakua* in front of your house for extra protection.

Graveyard and refinery

I HAVE A double-storey corner-house which faces the north and not far behind it is a beach. On the left is a graveyard and on the right, a few miles away is a refinery with a funnel that flames up at night. This scene is reflected in my sitting-room.

A friend of mine has mentioned that the refinery resembles a roaring dragon.

Dying
Negeri Sembilan

TO HAVE A property next to a beach is ideal, especially when it comes to recreation. However, since your house faces the north, which is a cold direction, you will not prosper financially.

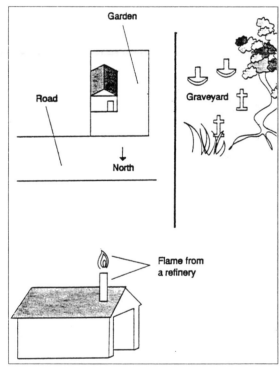

The damage to your house's feng shui is intensified by the grave yard next door. Since the graveyard is a place for the dead, your health and vitality will be sapped since you live so near it.

The flaming funnel which is reflected in your house only helps to stir up ghostly imaginations.

My advice is for you to sell off your property and live somewhere else with better feng shui.

PART
13

Houses

On stilts

MY HUSBAND AND I have been experiencing a lot of difficulties in our relationship. Our business ventures also seem to be going haywire.

Does this have anything to do with the fact that my house faces a reservoir and the back portion stands on concrete stilts?

LC
Kuala Lumpur

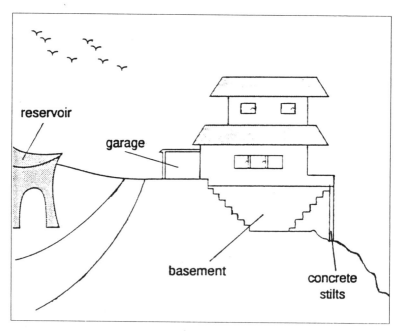

HAVING A RESERVOIR in front means a lot of opportunities coming your way but your dreams will not materialize.

Your house which is partly supported by concrete stilts is considered unlucky because it does not rest on properly balanced land.

Since the house is ill balanced, other things will also be unbalanced including your relationship with your husband.

The best solution is to sell the house. You may balance the house by filling the back with earth but I doubt it will be economically viable.

At cul-de-sac

MY HOUSE FACES the back of my neighbour's house. The main door is exactly opposite the living-room window. In such a situation, will my luck fly out?

I plan to build a fish-pond and install a water-pipe near the fence. Please advise.

Mr Chan
Sarawak

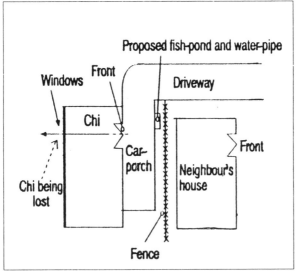

AS YOUR HOUSE is the last house at the end of the road, *chi* that comes in is less strong because other houses in front would have benefited from it first.

Having your main entrance facing the back of your neighbour's house is not too positive either, because it is an area where rubbish is normally disposed of.

Another negative point is that the main door of your house faces the living-room window. This will only worsen the feng shui because whatever remaining *chi* that seeps in will find a quick exit in that direction. Such a placing will only intensify the loss of wealth.

As a solution, build a wall in place of the fence so that it will cut off the unhealthy scene from the back of your neighbour's house.

As for the new pond and the water-pipe,

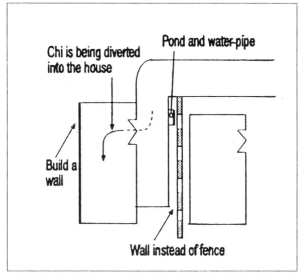

you may place it there to create some positive effects towards your house provided you replace the window with a solid wall so that *chi* the enters your house can be contained within.

L-shaped

I WAS FASCINATED by your weekly feng shui column during my recent visit to Malaysia.

Please advise me on the following:

☐ *My house is shaped in the form of an 'L'. How can I make it more stable?*

☐ *My driveway and the front lawn of my house slope downwards. How can I prevent my luck from running out?*

☐ *I have sleeping problems when I try to sleep with my feet facing the room door. How can I neutralize such a predicament?*

K.S. Tan
Victoria, Australia

IN FENG SHUI, your house which is shaped like an 'L' is also known as a shoe-shaped house. By having the main door too near the heel of the shoe-shaped house, good luck could be stamped out. To rectify this imbalance, have the main door placed further upwards.

Build a hump at the base of the slope of your driveway, to prevent wealth from draining away.

To have your feet facing the bedroom door is to have your *chi* and vitality drained off. Reposition your bed elsewhere in the room to restore harmony.

Boxes

I AM STAYING in my parent's house together with my youngest brother who is still single. I am married and have three sons.

Recently my sister-in-law moved back from Singapore. She has brought with her quite a number of furniture and personal belongings which are still unpacked and stacked in the house. Some of these furniture and boxes are kept in one corner of the living-room while some boxes are stacked up to the ceiling in the dining area. At the back of the house there are also a number of empty boxes which are stacked up in a shed.

Kindly advise whether such a living condition is good feng shui.

Helen Chong
Petaling Jaya

YOUR HOUSE IS filled with too many boxes and furniture. In feng shui, for a house to retain some harmony, it must not be filled to its brim with too many things as they are likely to retain *sha chi*. Try to clear out unnecessary empty boxes and have the useful items placed in a store-room.

PART
14

Apartments

Doors

I WOULD APPRECIATE it if you could give me your views on the following question:

In feng shui, which would you consider the main entrance to an apartment, the door that leads into the apartment, or the door that leads to the balcony?

I have also another question. How would you consider the feng shui of a block of apartments with:

☐ *The balconies facing a hill which is a mile away?*

☐ *The balconies facing a hill which is about 100 feet away?*

Peter Yong
Penang

A DOOR WHICH you use to enter an apartment, a house or a building is considered the main entrance, in feng shui as well as in everyday life. The main entrance can be considered the 'grand door' because it is the first door you go through in any premises.

So you cannot consider the balcony door of an apartment to be the main door unless you use that to enter, which is highly unlikely.

 As for your question about the hill: assuming that there are no other obstacles between the hills and your apartment, then the hill which is a mile away would not have much significance if it is a small one. If the hill is only 100 feet away, then the question of feng shui arises. If the feng shui direction from your balcony is good, then such a hill would definitely be an obstacle. If the feng shui direction is bad, then you are indeed lucky to have that hill as it acts as a shield for the occupants.

It is like watching a good movie or stage show. If you are far behind the crowd, then it would certainly not obstruct your view, so you may enjoy the show. If you are standing too near the crowd, it would block your view and deprive you of your enjoyment, just like an unwanted hill or mountain would stop the flow of good feng shui.

Staircase

*I HAVE AN apartment on the ground floor of the building with its main
door facing the stairs to the upper floor. Would it be all right to
continue using the main door, or should we use the side entrance,
which is through the kitchen?*

Madam Helen Tan
Kuala Lumpur

ACTUALLY, MADAM TAN, you are indeed very lucky to have your
apartment's main door facing the staircase leading to the upper floors.

It is definitely a positive sign because the stairs leading up may be taken to represent the steps towards progress in one's life. This symbolic upward movement augurs well in many endeavours, be it education, career or business.

On the other hand, having the main door of an apartment facing stairs that lead down is considered to be the reverse. The stairs leading down simply means the occupants will be dropping in status in life and society.

Luck was with you when you chose or were allotted this apartment, so thank your stars for this.

Quarry

I AM WORRIED about the effect in our family fortunes due to a quarry opposite the master bedroom of their apartment. We live on the third floor of a five-storey walk-up apartment. It is a corner-lot with the balcony of the master bedroom facing a quarry.

As far as we know, the quarry has not been very active and recently, it seems, some developer has proposed to develop high-rise apartments on top of the hill.

Is it considered bad feng shui to face a quarry? If so, what is the remedy?

Curious Flat Owner
Cheras

WELL, COMMON SENSE will tell you that when a person lives too near an active quarry, he puts his health at risk. You would notice it, of course, if after a while your lungs became badly affected by the dust that floats around the house. Those who are suffering from any respiratory ailments would find their illness compounded by the dust.

If the quarry is indeed to make way for a high-rise building, then the latter is the less harmful of the two.

Apart from putting up a *pakua* to deflect any ill luck, I do not see how you can improve the feng shui of your apartment as its position is fixed.

Faces north-east

THE MAIN ENTRANCE of the flat that I rent faces the north-east, which is also known as the Devil's Direction. It is not possible for me to move the main entrance elsewhere. Would it help to fix a pakua at the entrance? If so, where can I purchase such a mirror?

In Rooms 1 and 2, which position should I place my bed?

Lee Khek Kum
Shah Alam

THE MAIN ENTRANCE, situated at the front balcony of your flat, allows all the air to flow out through the other end of the balcony. You

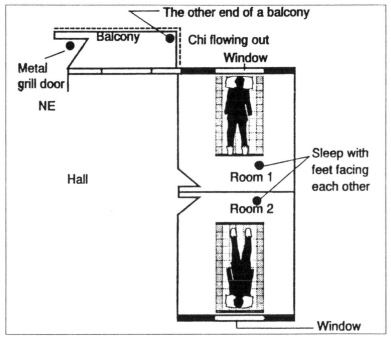

need not worry because negative *chi* will automatically zoom out in that direction instead of finding its way into your house.

A *pakua* normally acts as a deterrent when it is placed at the main entrance. It doesn't matter if the entrance has good or bad feng shui because it only reflects *sha chi* away. You can buy a *pakua* in Chinatown but it would be better to get the *hoi kong* from a reputed temple.

As for the bedrooms, you should place the back of the beds against the wall so that the windows are just above. The window above a person's head represents open skies, meaning that the sky's the limit.

Note that the occupants of both rooms should sleep with their feet facing each other as it symbolizes standing on a solid foundation.

Fronting south-west

IN AN EARLIER article you stated that a main door facing the south-west is said to face the Devil's Door. I wish to enquire whether this applies to apartments as well.

My apartment is on the sixth floor of a 13-storey block. The living-room and balcony face the south and the main entrance faces the south-west. Each floor has only five apartments, served by a central elevator.

Please advise me on the effects and any means of countering them.

Kevin Chong
Kuala Lumpur

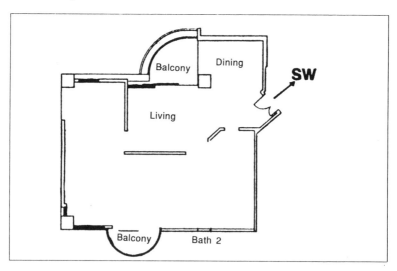

FROM THE DIAGRAM you provided, the living room and balcony face a good direction. The main entrance, however, faces the Devil's Back Door—to be precise—and this is not considered to be a good direction. Normally, people living in houses with the main door facing south-west do not get to enjoy life's goodness because their plans would always seem to go awry.

Changes can be recommended for a house but as your is in an apartment building, you may have to seek approval from the building management: this may not be easy to get.

The easiest way would be to reposition your entrance to face a different direction. The small space that has been created by this change of position may be used, say for storage of shoes.

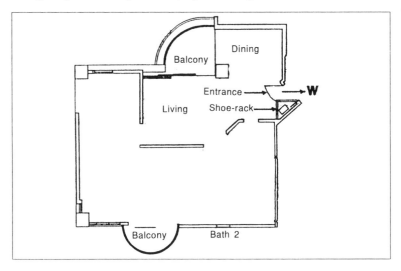

Faces south-west

WE LIVE ON the first floor of a low-cost flat. For the past three years, my husband has been jobless. We have two children. At the moment, I am the sole breadwinner. Please comment on the feng shui of our apartment.

Grateful

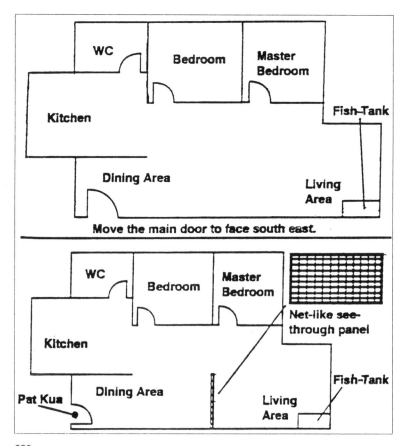

THE MAIN DOOR of your apartment faces the south-west which is known as the Devil's Back Door. To make matters worse, the fish-tank which symbolizes wealth is aligned with the main entrance. This means your wealth is literally stolen by the devil.

It would be best if you could carry out some renovations and change the position of the main door so that it faces the south-east. If this is not possible, then place a *pakua* on the main door to ward off negative *chi*.

As for the fish-tank, you could place an 8-foot wooden panel, with net-like designs, between the living-room and the dining area to 'catch' any wealth being siphoned away.

At odd angles

I LIVE IN an apartment with numerous odd angles and corners. I wonder what feng shui is there in store for such a case.

Teoh Heng Hua
Kuala Lumpur

SINCE YOU DID not give any sketch of how the "odd angles" in your apartment look like, I can only make an educated guess based on my own experiences with various properties.

Generally speaking, there are only two types of angles that can be found in the interior of a house or apartment. The first kind, the protruding angle, is like a triangle with one edge 'cutting' out of the wall like a knife. The second is the recessed angle.

To have too many angles in a home is considered bad feng shui because these shapes are considered 'fiery' ones. The presence of the fire element causes some imbalance in the family in terms of quarrels and backbiting.

The best remedy to 'extinguish' this fire in each case is:

☐ For the knife edge, place a tall potted plant in front of it to absorb the strong *chi* emanating from that point; and

☐ For the recessed angle, build a rack of cabinets or shelves to 'even out' the wall.

Knife shape

*I STAY On the first floor of a five-storey walk up apartment. The front
door of my apartment faces a staircase which leads upwards.*

*Ever since I moved into this apartment about one and a half years
ago, I have been unable to save any money. Friends tell me that it is*

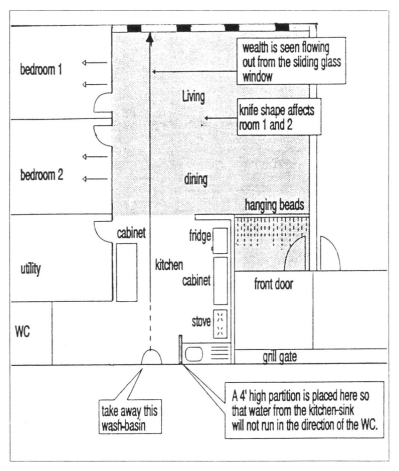

because of the direction of my stove which is in the same direction of the main door.

I understand that if the kitchen stove is facing such a direction the feng shui is 'no good'. Could you please help?

L.S. Lou
Kuala Lumpur

THE ILLUSTRATION SHOWS that your living and dining area has the shape of a knife whose sharp edge cuts into the two bedrooms, thus creating instability in the family.

To bring about some balance, place hanging beads to partition away the knife-handle so that the living-cum-dining room would resemble a rectangular shape.

As for your kitchen, your stove can remain where it is. However, as your wash-basin which is a source of wealth is in the direction of the sliding-window and the water-closet, much of your finances is being drained away. Besides, the kitchen is also found in the direction of the water-closet. To prevent such loss of wealth, remove the wash-basin and place a four-foot high plywood as shown in the diagram to act as a brake to store some wealth.

With a head

THE MAIN ENTRANCE of my new flat faces the south-west. Should I change the door so that it faces south-east?

Lawrence Low
Singapore

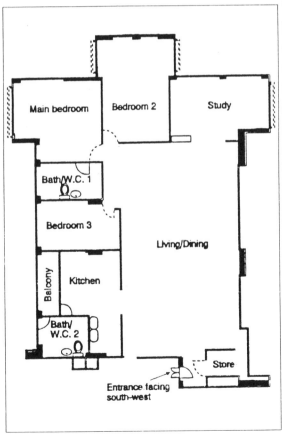

Entrance facing
south-west

THE MAIN
DOOR of your
entrance faces the
store-room, and
the south-west
direction which is
considered the
Devil's Back
Door. It would
help a lot to
change this
negative
alignment by
having your door
facing the
south-east.

As for the
shape of your
apartment, it is
the shape of a
person standing

upright with both arms outstretched. In feng shui, this is considered a positive shape. To reap the full benefit of this positive element, you might want to use Bedroom 2 as the main bedroom as it represents the head of a person.

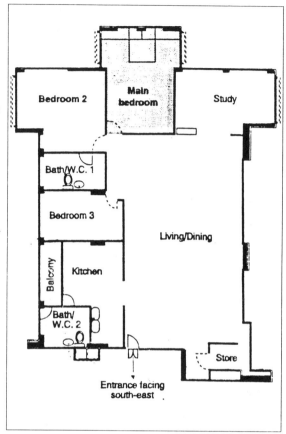

Bedroom 2

Main bedroom

Study

Bath/W.C. 1

Bedroom 3

Living/Dining

Balcony

Kitchen

Bath/ W.C. 2

Store

Entrance facing south-east

Next to a railway line

I WOULD LIKE to move my bed to another part of my room because of a leaking ceiling. There is some water seepage from the floor above (the bathroom of the flat upstairs is right over my room).

My upstairs neighbours are an unfriendly lot, so I need to move my bed before it becomes soaked through. I am also worried that if I position it wrongly, I may disrupt the flow of chi in my house.

Enclosed is a plan of my apartment which sits on high ground; railway tracks run parallel to the road in front of it. Two trees in front grow up to the second floor. My apartment faces west.

Mary
Kuala Lumpur

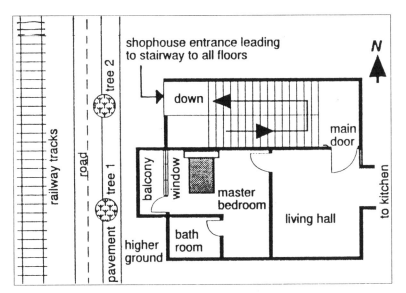

IF A HOUSE or an apartment ends up on the same level as a railway track, it is considered bad feng shui because the area is constantly 'shuddering' as trains pass by. In feng shui this symbolizes the foundations of your life being shaken. In your case, the apartment is on higher ground so the effect is lessened.

Another unfavourable point is that your apartment faces west, the White Tiger direction, which is not considered a good direction. Combined with the effect of the railway track, your apartment is considered to face a roaring tiger.

Besides hanging a *pakua* to keep the White Tiger at bay, nothing can actually be done.

As for your bed, it is currently in the best possible position. Since you find it difficult communicating with your upstairs neighbour, hire a contractor yourself to patch up the leaking ceiling as soon as possible.

Cable

I LIVE ON the highest level of a five-storey apartment. From my balcony, I can see high-tension cables.

Since moving in, we have found that we have never had any luck. Can you please advise?

Ho Kok Shung
Kuala Lumpur

THE MAIN DOOR is often regarded as the most important door of a house as it is the first door that leads one into one's house.

The best solution in this case is to move house. Otherwise place a pair of metal scissors on the left- and right-hand side of the entrance to 'cut off' the negative pylon.

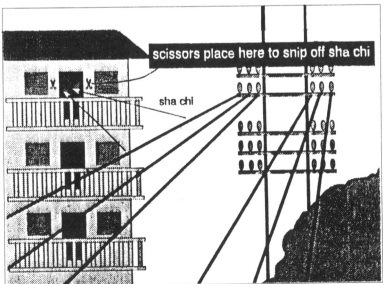

Lighting

I WOULD BE grateful if you could advise me on the following:
☐ *Would the glaring light of the sun from the skylight affect the occupant of a room which has no windows? If it does, how can I create a better harmony without having to alter anything in the room?*
☐ *Is it good to have a very bright interior for the home?*

Julia Lim
Penang

A BEDROOM THAT has no window is not an ideal place for resting as natural air or *chi* cannot flow in to ventilate it. One can say that this kind of room has no life. Secondly, as the room gets a lot of sunlight during the day, this would naturally heat up the room, making it unconducive to sleep in at night. To create harmony, you would have to change something, thus renovating is necessary.

As for the skylight, it could be replaced with tiles to prevent the sunlight from coming in. Whether it is for a house or a building, the story is still the same when it comes to having artificial or natural lightings. That is to say, to find harmony, one's place must not be in total brightness or in pure darkness.

For instance, dim lighting may be necessary to create an atmosphere of cosiness for the living-room and bright lights would be more suitable for the study to prevent eye-strain. Thus to find a proper balance, a place must have light and darkness in its rightful place.

130

Tunnel

MY FAMILY AND I live in a flat which faces a mountain with a tunnel at the top. We find that despite all efforts, personal goals seem to elude us.

Anonymous
Penang

THERE IS NOT much prosperity in store for you if your house faces a tunnel. It is best that you shift to a new environment for a change of luck. If that is not possible, place a *pakua* facing the tunnel to counter its forces.

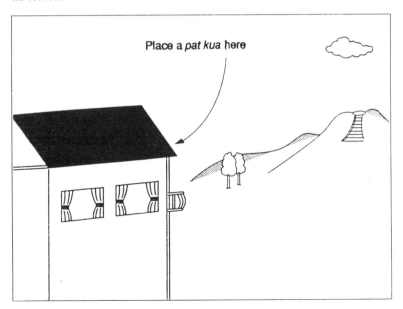

When fire and
wealth clash

I HAVE BEEN living on the eighth floor of an apartment building for the past two and half years. Generally things are fine except we find it hard to save because of repairs on the house.

Madam Khoo
Penang

THE MAIN CULPRIT behind your family's woes is the bathroom. It is in the shape of a triangle, which connotes the Fire Element. Since the bathroom symbolizes a source of wealth, to have it clash with the Fire Element would cause money problems.

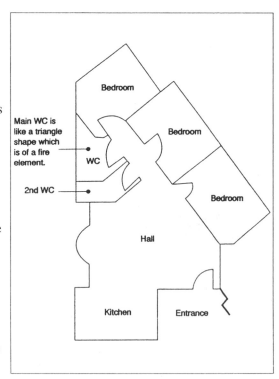

Since the shape of your main bathroom cannot be changed, it is best that your family not use it. Use the second water-closet which is of a more neutral shape.

Uneven flow of *chi*

I AM LIVING on the first floor of a shophouse which has three bedrooms, a kitchen and a sitting-room. Do you have any advice for the layout of the furniture in my room?

Viven Chen
Kuching

BY HAVING YOUR bed above the stairway and your windows parallel with each other, your sleep is being overrun by vicious *chi* from the bottom and the top.

To overcome this uneven flow, seal up one of the windows. Secondly, place the bed on the other side of the room with the computer table by its side.

Have the bedroom door opening on the left instead of the right so that it will not 'cut' part of the bed in two when it is left open. Lastly, the cupboard and the ironing-table can be placed on the other side of the bedroom.

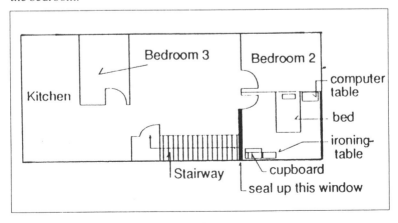

Breaking the curse

SINCE MOVING INTO this apartment a year ago, my marriage and family have broken up. My business venture has also failed. I am now jobless and alone.

Did my sleeping position have anything to do with my present situation?

Desperate
Kuala Lumpur

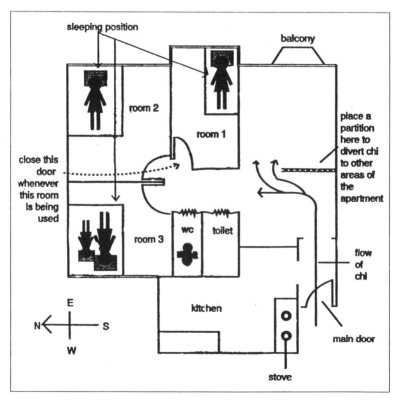

AS THERE IS a balcony facing your main door, a lot of your good luck has 'run away' unnecessarily. You can control this outward flow of *chi* by placing a wooden partition so that *chi* would be diverted to other areas of the apartment.

See the diagram for the suggested arrangements of Rooms 1, 2 and 3; the door of Room 1 should be closed because it faces the toilet. As your stoves (a Fire Element) are near the position of north (the Water Element area), there would be a conflict, thus destroying your wealth.

For better harmony, remove your stoves and place them in a position facing south (the Fire Element area).

Clothes-line at entrance

MY HUSBAND AND I live in a small flat, and since moving in we have been experiencing bad luck. We face financial difficulties and recently, we missed out on our promotions in the company, even though we worked very hard.

Could all these have something to do with the feng shui of our flat?

**S.H. Tan
Penang**

YOUR MAIN ENTRANCE faces the clothes-line outside the flat: in feng shui, this symbolizes

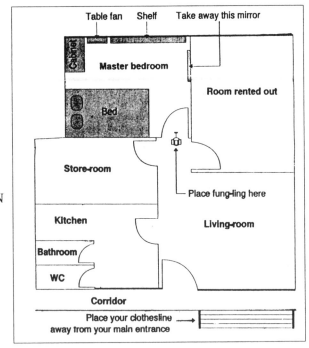

that the entrance has been cut off. As a result, you will not go far in your career or in life. You can enhance your luck by placing the clothes-line further away from the entrance.

The mirror in your room can be removed elsewhere so that it would not 'siphon' *chi* away from you when you are asleep. I notice that your bedroom door in aligned with the main door: this too is bad feng shui. Place a *feng ling* (wind-chime) at your bedroom doorway to slow down the movement of *chi* in and out of your flat.

PART
15

The Pakua

Fixing it and its usage

AFTER READING YOUR article on how to ward off bad luck with the use of a pakua, I rushed out and bought one. It has been a long time since I hung it at the front door of my house, but nothing has changed. Can you tell me what could have gone wrong?

LLN
Selangor

IF YOU HAD read my earlier article properly, you would have a fairly good idea of what a mirror or a *pakua* should do.

As I mentioned then, a mirror would only attract light, energy or *chi*—which is neither good nor bad—in your direction. On the other hand, an ordinary *pakua* bought off the street will work the same as a mirror unless it has been *hoi kong* (had its 'eye opened'). Similarly, any talisman bought from a street vendor is useless unless it is blessed by a spiritual man. In this context, to *hoi kong* a *pakua* is to charge it with *chi* so that, once it is hung at an appropriate spot, it will reflect whatever unwanted *chi* that comes in your direction.

If you have trouble finding someone to *hoi kong* the *pakua* for you, go to a nearby temple and ask around. You may find someone adept in this kind of work to do it for you.

In your letter, you also said that you hung the *pakua* at the front door. Now, the proper position for it is over the doorway. If you hung it on the door itself, then problems might arise because whenever the door is opened and left open, the *pakua* would not be in a position to do its work.

Without giving the *pakua* a good permanent place to hang, your fortune may be inconsistent.

Blocked *pakua*

*I HAD PLACED my pakua above the main door of my house. But later
when I discovered that it was partially blocked by a sloping roof, I
repositioned it. Have I done the right thing?*

Mrs Chan
Kuching

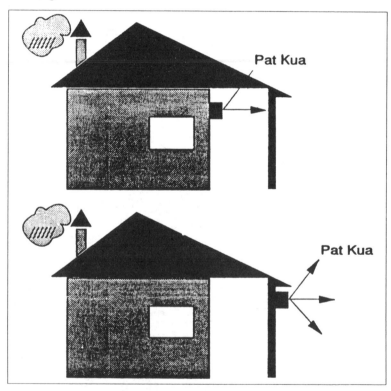

WHEN YOU DECIDE to place a *pakua* in your house, you should see
to it that the *pakua* is not obstructed by anything. Otherwise, this will

defeat the purpose of having the *pakua* there in the first place. Yes, you have done the right thing by placing your *pakua* further out so that it can reflect the unwanted elements that come your way.

Pakua or mirror

THE MAIN DOOR of my house is blocked by a row of trees. I have put up a plain mirror to reflect things. After reading an earlier article of yours, regarding the difference between a plain mirror and a pakua, I began to have second thoughts about the mirror. Should I replace it? How do I 'energize' a pakua?

Boong Kim Kiew
Penang

BECAUSE YOUR INTENTION is to reflect the trees that block your entrance, you should use a *pakua* instead of a mirror. By using a mirror, you actually intensify problems heading in your direction. For a *pakua* to do the job it should be energized before it is used, or it is just a plain mirror performing the wrong function.

Energizing a *pakua* is also called *hoi kong* in Chinese, or "opening the eye". When this is properly done, it reflects all unwanted things that are deemed as obstacles. There are a few ways to *hoi kong* a *pakua*, but the art of doing it is a closely guarded trade secret.

What you can do is that perhaps, when you buy your *pakua* from any shop that sells such items, you should take it to a reputable Chinese temple for a priest to do the *hoi kong* before using it for your house.

Invoking its powers

I HAVE JUST bought a double-storey link-house that faces the south-west. How good or bad is this in terms of feng shui and how can I counter the bad chi.

I am also uncertain about the use of the pakua. Can I take care of unwanted chi simply by placing a pakua in the direction of the source of bad chi?

Are there any rules to be observed in putting up a pakua?

E.H. Lim
Petaling Jaya

A main entrance that faces south-west is deemed to be the Devil's Back Door. If you can, renovate the house so that your main entrance faces another direction. If not, you can use the *pakua*.

In putting up the *pakua*, you should get a medium to perform the necessary rituals. Otherwise, the mirror would not serve its purpose.

Faces *pakua*

MY FLAT IS located on the ninth floor. The main door faces the bedroom door of my flat neighbour. On top of his door is a pakua. What is the effect of the pakua on my family?

Lim Boo San
Butterworth

THE REASON YOUR neighbour placed a *pakua* above his bedroom door is probably because your main entrance faces his room. Since a *pakua* normally deflects *sha chi*, this may cause you some disharmony.

To solve your problem, talk to your neighbour diplomatically and ask him to take down the *pakua* since he may have unintentionally placed it there.

Alternatively, you may place a *feng ling* (wind-chime) at your door so that the swift *chi* can be slowed down: harmony in your home will thus be preserved.

140

Queries

TYPICAL READERS' QUESTIONS on *pakua*:

☐ *What type of pakua should I buy if I need to use one?*
Ordinary *pakua*, an eight-sided trigram, normally has a mirror placed in the middle of it. Some do not have a mirror but come with other symbols, like the circular yin and yang. In fact, in this day and age, it is not surprising to come across many unusual *pakua* designs. However, the traditional forms of *pakua* have been tried and tested through the ages, so it is advisable to use these varieties rather than the modern ones.

☐ *After buying a pakua, do I have to choose an auspicious day to hang it up?*
For total effectiveness, choosing an auspicious date and time to hang up a *pakua* would be wise; after all, there is a time for everything under the heavens. If you want to do something, why not do it properly?

☐ *Does one have to put up a pakua over all the doors allowing entry into a house, or just the main door?*
This depends on the overall situation of the house.

Cannon

I REFER TO an earlier article of yours in which you advised a reader to use a pakua to correct the imbalances of an 'artificial mountain' which faces his house, and which had adversely affected his financial situation.

My house is also located opposite a row of houses built on higher ground. This has put me in the same financial predicament as the earlier reader. However, for various reasons, it is not possible for me to put a pakua in front of my house.

Is there another alternative, short of moving to another house?

K.Y. Lee
Penang

THE EASIEST WAY to ward off undesirable influences is to put up a *pakua*. In fact, the *pakua* is one of the most used instruments in warding off bad *chi*, evil spirits, etc.

If you fear that you may be ridiculed for putting up the *pakua*, then perhaps you might like to put up a cannon instead, to symbolize the act of blasting away bad elements. Just think again, you have nothing to lose by putting up the *pakua*. The advantages to be gained should outweigh any fears of ridicule.

PART
16

Shapes

Heavenly shaped land

I AM HAVING my new house designed in a circular shape because I think it is unique. However, I have received some positive and negative comments from my friends regarding its feng shui. Please advise.

Elizabeth Ng
Johor Bahru

BY ITSELF, A circular form is also known as the "heavenly shape" in feng shui. Some temples are structured along this line because the shape gives off good *chi*. However, houses are unlike temples which use the whole interior as one room. The rooms insides a circular house usually end up having odd shapes. Since uneven shapes create uneven *chi*, disharmony in the family may be the consequence.

The best thing to do is to secure a professional feng shui consultant to help you arrange your rooms in an auspicious area, leaving the insignificant rooms tucked in the odd nooks.

Bucket-shaped land

I ENCLOSED A sketch of my lot with its nearby surroundings, as I plan to build a house there. Can you give tips on a good direction for the house?

Levita Michael
Sabah

FROM YOUR SKETCH, I note that your plot of land is bucket-shaped. Because of its unique shape, your house should ideally face the mouth of the 'bucket' to enable good fortune to flow in. This would place your house facing north. In feng shui, the north (Black Tortoise area) is not generally a good direction for the house to face as invisible obstacles are believed to come from there.

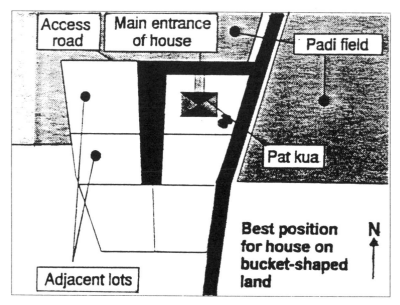

Therefore it may seem ironic for me to ask you to build your house facing north. But in feng shui, each case has to be studied individually. In view of your bucket-shaped lot, north is the best direction for your house to face. Still, I would advise you to put a *pakua* there to counter any negative forces and achieve harmony with Nature.

Odd-shaped land

I READ IN one of your articles that a land shape which is wider at the back and narrower in front is bad feng shui.

Well, my house lot is exactly that shape. I tend to believe your theory because even though my husband and I are considered by many to be in the high income brackets, we are actually quite broke.

I would like to mention too that I'm very unlucky when it comes to lotteries. Over the past seven years, on two occasions I have had the joy of winning a consolation prize only to discover in the following day's newspaper that my winning number was but an error.

Feeling Broke
Sungai Petani

I NOTE FROM your sketch that your house is a corner-lot. Most corner-lots have odd shapes where the back portion is bigger than the front. Since the shape of the land cannot be altered, you can plant a row of trees to create the illusion of a rectangular shape. This would bring about some balance and

Land having a wider back

Land with a narrow front

HOUSE

Gate

A land with a narrow front and a wider back often finds it hard to contain any money.

enhance the feng shui of your house.

Since lady luck is not with you where gambling is concerned, I would advise you not to waste your time and money chasing after that elusive jackpot.

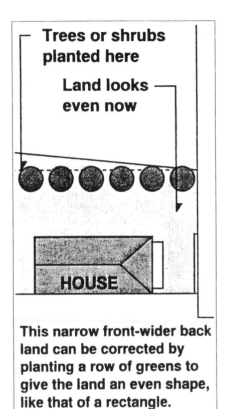

Trees or shrubs planted here

Land looks even now

HOUSE

This narrow front-wider back land can be corrected by planting a row of greens to give the land an even shape, like that of a rectangle.

Axe-shaped land

I READ IN one of your articles that it is no good feng shui to have your house sitting on a plot of land shaped like a knife. It seems too that one should not paint one's house red.

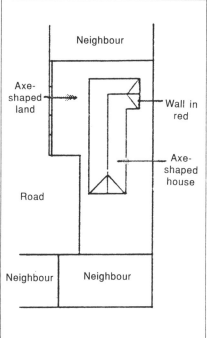

Enclosed is a sketch of my house plan. Can you please advice?

Mrs Shirley Yap
Melaka

YOUR LAND IS actually axe-shaped, with the sharp edge on the other side of the compound. In this arrangement where the house has an identical shape, but in the opposite direction, it symbolizes a struggle for authority.

To paint the edge of the axe red would only intensify the problem. If the wall is part of the store-room, then the problem would not be so bad. But its a definite no-no for a bedroom or living-room, in which case the wall should be painted white.

If you intend to do some major renovation, you can have the back of your house extended in a straight line, as shown in the diagram. You

can build a porch in the front
portion of your house, so that it
fits in just nicely with the
axe-shaped piece of land.

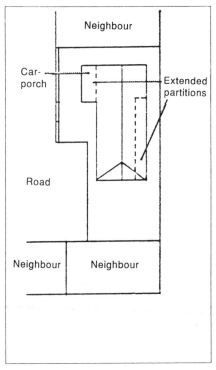

Pointed garden

MY FAMILY AND I live in a semi-detached house that faces south. It has a 'pointed' garden and two entrances.

Purely for convenience, we use the back entrance more often. Is it considered bad feng shui to have a 'pointed' garden?

Mrs Y. Chin
Ipoh

IN FENG SHUI, Mrs Chin, a triangular shape is not regarded as 'pointed' but falls under the Fire Element. So you could say that part of your land is in the 'land of fire'.

Consider it a blessing in disguise that your house is not built over that triangular stretch of the land or you may not find peace at home because living on 'fiery land' will only cause quarrels and misunderstandings. What you could do is grow trees in a straight line

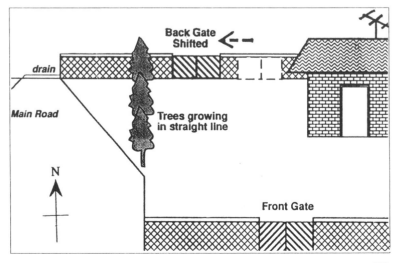

from the right-angled edge of your property (see diagram). This would cut off the 'fiery' portion of your land, which itself may be beautified by planting flowers around it. You would also find that by doing so, your house is on a land that is more balanced in shape.

You also mentioned that for convenience, you and your family use the back gate instead of the front. May I suggest that you use a longer route and take the front gate because that direction (south) is better in terms of feng shui than going through the back gate (north).

Your diagram indicates that your front and back gates 'overlap' each other slightly. I would suggest that you move your back gate further to the left so they do not overlap.

Blades of
double-axe

MY HUSBAND AND I run a direct sales business from our house. However, business is just moderate and fortune does not seem to be coming our way. I wonder if this factor could be due to the tree opposite my house or the arrangement of furniture in my hall.

S.H. Ooi
Petaling Jaya

THE TREE OPPOSITE your house is not a contributing factor to your bad feng shui. But looking at the arrangement of the furniture, your problem can be traced to the cupboard where your products are displayed. You will see that as your sitting/dining area is T-shaped,

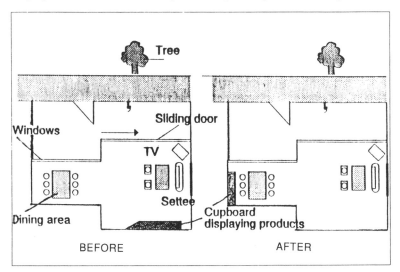

what is called "double-axe" in feng shui, putting your products at one of the 'blade' edges only serves to destroy them.

To enhance your business, it is advisable for you to rearrange your display cupboard closer to the dining area; this is the 'axe handle' and so you will have better control of things. Secondly, because the area is the place where meals are taken, it would also symbolize the constant availability of food for your family.

Land next to river

RECENTLY I BOUGHT a house which faces the east and has a river running beside it. As the compound is large, I intend to plant durian trees and perhaps rear fish in an outdoor pond. Can you please advise?

Khoo Teng Lee
Butterworth

A HOUSE LOCATED near a cul-de-sac is generally considered undesirable. A river running besides it can make a difference in generating new life.

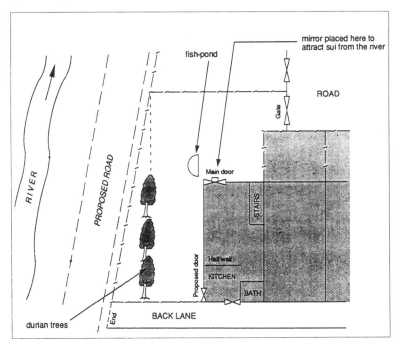

However, since the river does not run towards your main entrance, wealth (*sui*) is flowing away from your house. To put a stop to this, place an ordinary round mirror at the top of your main door to attract *sui*.

Plant your durian trees parallel to your house to create balance on the land. It would be ideal to place your fish-pond by the side of the main entrance to welcome luck and fortune.

Split-level house

MADAM WONG YOKE Ngo of Petaling Jaya was told that if a house is built with a split level and there are five steps from one level to the next, it would signify a 'descent into hell'.

Furthermore, she has heard that a house placed at a cul-de-sac is not too well positioned because the *chi* from the main road would swiftly penetrate the building. The result, as she was told, would be illness and bad luck, especially if the main door of the house faces the main road.

Well, in feng shui, it is often considered that a house should not be built on a split level where one enters at the upper level and then has to

descent to get to the rest of the house. This is seen as being symbolic of a demotion. If a houseowner does not want to regress in life, career or business, it is best that he chooses a house with steps leading up rather than down from the entrance level. The matter about 'descend into hell' is pure nonsense cooked up by some over-imaginative mind. Don't get carried away by it.

To the other question concerning the house on the cul-de-sac, it is indeed true that a house at the end of a road is not very favourable in its feng shui. The *chi* travelling along that path would have been taken up by the other houses along the way.

If the main door faces the main road, then it is considered to be similar to a T-junction because it takes the full force of the *chi* coming from the road. If your house happens to be in such a position, what you can do is change the facing of your main door so that it does not receive the direct thrust of the *chi* flow. To balance out the effect of being the last house to receive the benefits of the *chi*, you can build a fountain, pond or swimming pool as it is widely held that these 'watery' structures help to generate *chi* in places where it may be naturally lacking.

Snake formation

I HAVE BEEN living in my present house for the past nine years. Since shifting in, I have been having financial and business difficulties. Enclosed is a plan of my house. Can you advise?

Lim Choon Teck
Kuala Lumpur

THE DIAGRAM SHOWS that yours is a split-level house where the kitchen is lower that the hall. This is called the "snake formation" in feng shui, and bears a negative influence on the occupants. Such negativeness can be in the form of a business failure or a demotion in one's career.

Since you cannot level the flooring of the kitchen to that of your hall, place mirrors on the ceiling of your kitchen to balance the *chi* in the hall and the kitchen.

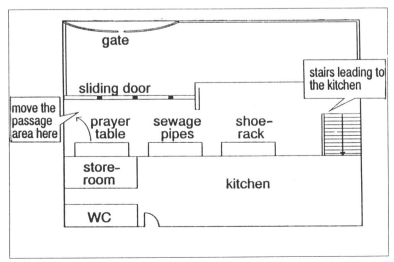

PART
17

Driveways and Porches

Sailing

I HAVE A house with a porch curving upwards. The design of the main gate peaks at the centre. I would like to know their implications in feng shui.

Eric Lau
Ipoh

YOUR MAIN GATE, with sharp points in the centre, bears no adverse implications as the sharp *chi* is sent shooting skywards without harming anyone.

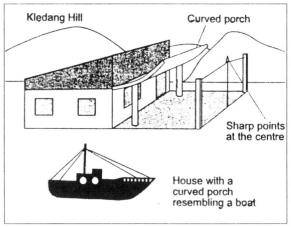

Kledang Hill

Curved porch

Sharp points at the centre

House with a curved porch resembling a boat

Now, your curved porch sounds interesting. Such structures are usually found in villages or towns dominated by fishermen. Hence fishing is the main occupation. Let's assume that the sea is nearby too.

Fishing is an unpredictable occupation in that the fishermen are at the mercy of the weather. They are exposed to the elements of nature, especially the wind. The wind can be helpful at times but it can also threaten their lives by stirring up giant waves. Therefore fishermen would always pray that the wind would be merciful to them at sea, so that they can have a bountiful haul.

Some wealthy fishermen build their houses in the shape of boats as signified by the upwardly curving porch, to show that even on land, they would have

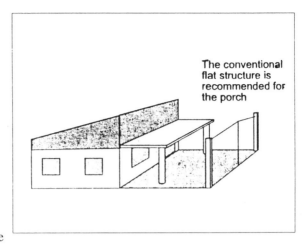

The conventional flat structure is recommended for the porch

smooth sailing. But your house being built with such a shape may bring problems since it is situated inland.

In feng shui, we can say that your ship is sailing on land, thus retarding one's progress in life. To take advantage of such a shape, you have to make sure that your house is situated near water.

Perhaps it would be better for you to alter the shape of your porch to the conventional flat structure.

Sloping

I BOUGHT A second-hand house five years ago. It is a corner-lot and near a road junction. The driveway to the garage is located on a slope.

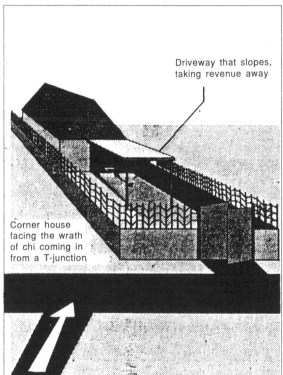

Driveway that slopes, taking revenue away

Corner house facing the wrath of chi coming in from a T-junction

Ever since I moved in, my family and I have been plagued by bad luck. I suffer from ill health, and I have lost most of my savings too. I used to be lucky but not anymore.

Jay
Kuala Lumpur

AS YOUR CORNER-LOT house is too near a road junction, bad *chi* coming from that direction could bring misfortune to your household. You can remedy the situation by placing a *pakua* in front of your house, or you can plant a tree or two at the corner of the garden to ward off the *sha chi*.

Your driveway, which slopes down to the main road is the main culprit of your financial downfall. Level up the driveway to bring about financial stability in your home.

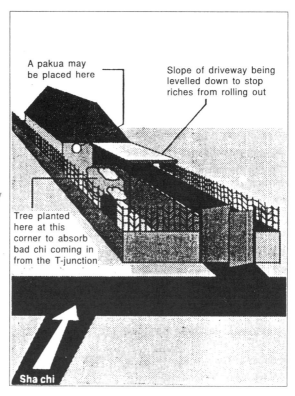

A pakua may be placed here

Slope of driveway being levelled down to stop riches from rolling out

Tree planted here at this corner to absorb bad chi coming in from the T-junction

Sha chi

Blowpipe

I HAVE EXTENDED my porch, using a simple awning consisting of iron pipes and sheets of asbestos. Lately, I have pushed the asbestos sheets a bit higher, and by doing so, the iron pipes with their exposed hollow ends seem to point towards my house. I am afraid that this may bring ill fortune to my family.

What do you suggest?

Freddy Tan
Klang

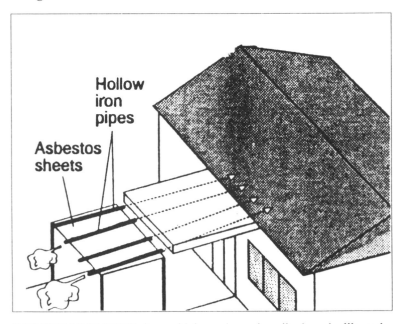

THE HOLLOW IRON pipes which you have described can be likened to blowpipes. As both ends of the pipes are open, *sha chi* can go in from either direction. Thus it is bad luck as *sha chi* can easily be diverted towards your house.

To neutralize this bad influence, perhaps you could seal up the ends of the pipes as shown in the diagram.

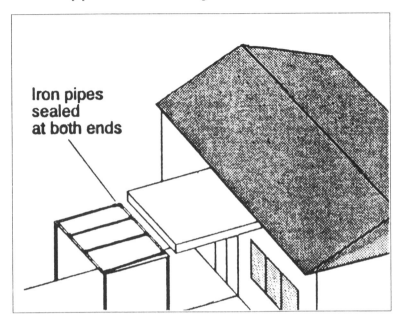

**Iron pipes
sealed
at both ends**

Black car

I HAVE A big black car which blocks half the driveway in my house. Would this block chi from coming into my house?

Also, there is a gutter at the front and back portions of the roof edge, to carry away rain-water. Would this structure affect the feng shui of my house?

Big Black Car
Kuala Lumpur

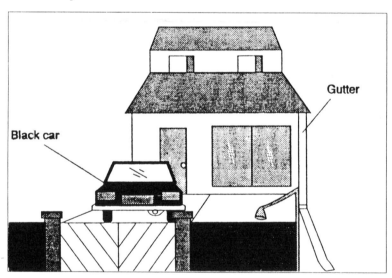

NO, YOUR CAR would not be blocking *chi* from entering your house. The gutter serves a very practical purpose. In fact, it might even be good for the feng shui of your house as it prevents rain-water from splashing in, since you do not have an awning in front.

Cable

*I LIVE IN a single-storey terraced house in Ipoh. There is a low
overhead Rediffusion cable which passes just above my car-porch. Are
there any negative effects from the cable? Lately, I notice that luck
seems to be eluding me.*

Very Curious
Ipoh

TO HAVE THE whole compound, including the pathway from your
gate into your house, being 'cut' by a cable is to have your initial luck
cut off. If you want better luck, you might have to disconnect the cable.

Green turf

I AM THINKING of cementing the garden outside my house. Will this affect the feng shui of my residence?

Jenny Foo
Kelantan

IF YOUR CAR-PORCH already has tiles and some concrete form of flooring, it is better to leave the garden in its natural state. Otherwise, if the whole compound is cemented up, the heat of the sun may be reflected towards your house which may be too hot for comfort.

Low pigeon-holed wall

*I AM
PLANNING
to shift my
garage to the
right side of
the house.
Would this
be a good
move in feng
shui?*

**Mr Yong
Kuala Lumpur**

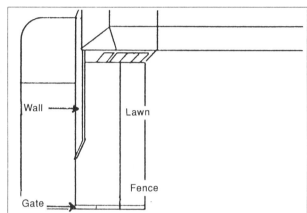

BY MOVING THE garage to the right, this would create more space

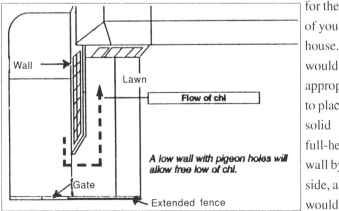

for the front of your house. But it would not be appropriate to place a solid full-height wall by the side, as this would block the free flow of *chi*. If you need to put a wall there, it should be a low wall, with pigeon-holes in them to allow *chi* to come in.

Roofs

Rolling into the sea

I SEEM TO have no luck at all. Can you kindly comment on the feng shui of my house?

Lim Lum Teo
Penang

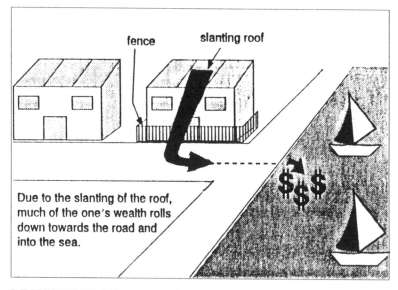

fence   slanting roof

Due to the slanting of the roof, much of the one's wealth rolls down towards the road and into the sea.

LIVING NEAR AN ocean can be considered lucky if your house faces the water. However, as the roof of your house slants towards the road, much of your luck is rolling out towards the sea.

To net back some of your resources place grilles at the windows, main door and fence.

Air-wells

FROM SEREMBAN, C.H. Low has sent us a question on air-wells and multilevelled roofs. He has been told that both types of structures are not good in terms of feng shui as they represent mental disorders and poor health.

Mr Low, getting advice from a layman who knows only half the facts in feng shui always brings a great risk with it. Instead of helping you, it may end up giving you more problems.

I have yet to come across any case where an air-well in the house makes the occupants go crazy. In a warm country like ours, an air-well is even desirable for ventilation purposes. Feng shui theory also states that the balanced house must have sufficient ventilation so that *chi* flowing in and out can benefit its occupants.

When a house has too many openings in the form of doors and windows, good *chi* coming in may be dispersed too quickly before it

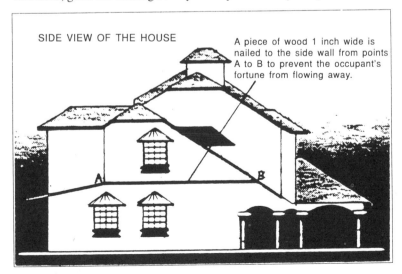

SIDE VIEW OF THE HOUSE

A piece of wood 1 inch wide is nailed to the side wall from points A to B to prevent the occupant's fortune from flowing away.

can do any good. So a large house must have more windows and a small house should have fewer.

As for the multilevelled roof, the diagram you sent us would indicate that your problem would be one of fortune flowing away quickly since the roof has a steep slope. You don't need to carry out any extensive renovation; just nail an inch-thick piece of wood running across the side of the house to block the total erosion of your luck.

Knife-shaped land and sloping roof

MY HOUSE HAS a long sloping roof. I recall in one of the earlier articles that such a roof will cause fortunes to flow away. I seem to lose whatever profits I make.

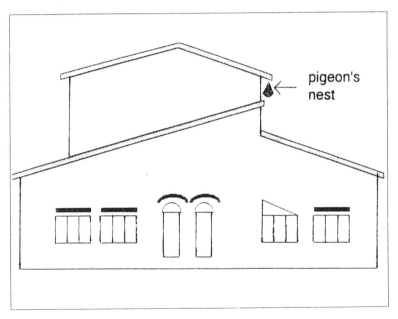

pigeon's nest

As the external walls have rough plastered surfaces, it may be quite difficult to nail wood strips on them.

There is a pigeon's nest on the roof too. Please advise.

Mrs C.C. Chan
Kuching

YOUR HOUSE IS sitting on a weak site as shown by the knife-shaped land. To restore balance, take away the wooden gate to give your house a rectangular land to sit on.

A cross-section of your house reveals that the slopes of the roofs do not balance, so it is difficult for wealth to remain in the family. To correct this, you need major renovation to raise the lower roof as shown in the diagram.

One of your windows has an odd slant. Change it so that it is in uniform with the rest. Remove the pigeon's nest from your roof-top too.

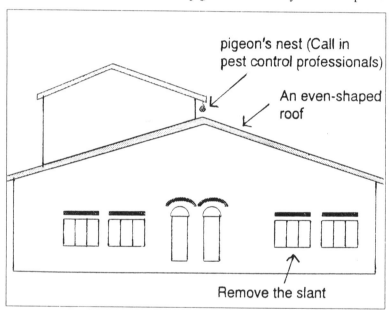

pigeon's nest (Call in pest control professionals)

An even-shaped roof

Remove the slant

Solar water heater

MY HUSBAND WAS told by some friends that putting a solar water heater on the roof of the house is considered bad feng shui because it is like opening a hole and allowing good fortune and chi to flow out. What do you think?

Mrs Amy Lim
Ampang

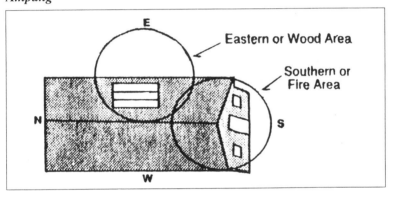

TECHNOLOGY MAY BRING new wonders and tools but the principles of feng shui remain constant. Because the heater derives its energy directly from the sun, we can say that it is symbolic of the fire element.

Good locations for the heater are the east and south; east represents the Wood Element, which is important for fire, and south is the direction of the Fire Element.

As for the question of whether or not the solar heater would be detrimental to your good fortune, bear in mind that the opening created for the device is no different in terms of feng shui than an air-well. So there should not be any worry about your luck flowing away.

PART
19

Colours

Choosing of colours

DO THE COLOURS red or black have any bearing on feng shui, if they are used on a car? Are there any good colours to choose for a car?

Interested Person
Penang

YOU MUST ALWAYS understand that there is no colour which can really be considered bad. You must use your own discretion to judge what is good for yourself. For instance, if a person is quick to lose his temper and gets angry at the slightest annoyance, he should not use red too often. This is like adding fuel to the fire.

If you are observant enough and have the time to spare, wait at a convenient spot and you may observe that most drivers of red cars tend to speed—no offence to those who drive red cars. As red is a very powerful and energetic colour, it would be all right for a timid person to wear that colour—it enhances his courage to do things more confidently and positively.

Most important of all, understand your character and the power of colours before applying them to your life—lest they control you!

Neutral colours

I LIVE IN a house which faces north and has its doors, gates and window grilles painted red and black. The back door of the house, which faces south, has a brown door. How can I get around this?

Worried
Penang

TO MINIMIZE YOUR problem, change the colour of your gates, doors and grilles to a more neutral colour. Why not paint the gates and doors light yellow or brown, and the grilles white? I believe that after a while things at home will be more in harmony for you and your family.

Door

MY HUSBAND AND I will be moving into a new apartment soon. My husband has painted the frame of the front door (on the outside) black and the door itself yellow. From the inside, he has painted the frame red and the door white.

I want to know if this combination of colours is proper.

PCW

THE COLOUR COMBINATION you and your husband chose is certainly a strange one. Since you did not mention the direction which the door faces, I can only give you a superficial reply.

To me, this combination of colours is unique and overdone. The effects can be confusing. Furthermore, the colours red and black are

not normally in harmony with each other especially in this situation when they are placed back to back.

You also have to watch out if you are the type who entertains a lot. Because red is also the colour for "stop": you don't need to wonder why your guests seem reluctant to leave when the party is over.

As a suggestion, and from a more practical viewpoint, why not just pain the frame of the door dark brown and the main door light brown? I believe it would give your entrance a very natural look.

Apple green

I RECENTLY GOT married and my marriage life is not running smoothly and I am also facing health problems.

Has it got something to do with the layout of my house?

GKT
Kuala Lumpur

WHENEVER THE MAIN door is opened it will slam the wall which will vibrate your bed head on the other side of the wall. This will definitely put your marriage into deep trouble. Place your bed on the opposite side of your room.

Painting your room apple green would also help bring harmony to your marriage as the colour has a calming effect.

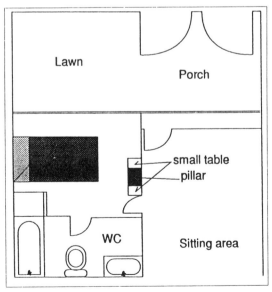

Red wall

HAVING MOVED RECENTLY into a rented apartment, I find that I am becoming easily irritated by minor problems. I cannot concentrate on my schoolwork and my father's health is deteriorating.

I wonder if the red wall facing my apartment is the root of all my problems.

Lim Lek Kneah
Sungai Nibong

THE COLOUR RED gives off a vibrant active and hot energy. To have an apartment facing a six-storey wall of that colour is to have trouble. Red adds fuel to one's aura. No wonder you find yourself and your family members touchy and irritable.

If you can, move away from this place. If not, place a *pakua* at your front door and have all the glass windows tinted light blue. Placing some pots of green plants along the corridor would also help absorb the 'fire' coming from the red wall.

PART
20

Mirrors

Mirror magic

YOU MENTIONED THAT a pakua is to disperse bad chi while an ordinary mirror is to attract light and positive chi. Is it wise then to have lots of mirrors in the house to bring in positive chi?

Can you recommend a place in the house where I can put up all those mirrors?

Danny Chan
Kuala Lumpur

IT IS CORRECT that a *hoi kong pakua* always deflects unwanted *chi* while an ordinary mirror attracts light and positive *chi*. But the mirror is like any other tool: you must know how to handle it properly to enable it to serve its purpose.

Therefore if your house faces a pond, lake or ocean, a mirror placed in the hall to reflect such images in the interior will bring positive effects to the owner because water means money. However, if you place a mirror wrongly and it attracts bad images into your home, then you will have bad luck.

On the wall

THERE IS A large show-case with attached mirror facing the front door and window of my house.

Recently, some visitors suggested that I should remove the mirror from the show-case. However after some thought, I

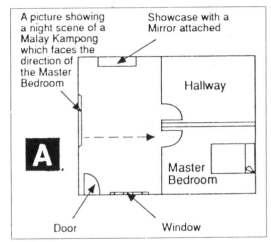

am now thinking of placing the show-case in front of the master bedroom door.

I would also like to know whether a picture depicting a night scene in a kampong has any bearing on the feng shui of my home.

Madam Wong Siew Key
Butterworth

WELL, MADAM WONG, since there have not been any major upheavals in your household all this time, the show-case could be left in the same position that it has been occupying all along.

Removing the mirror is entirely up to you. To have a mirror on a wall facing the main door can be either positive or negative, depending on what is in front of your house. For example, if your house faces

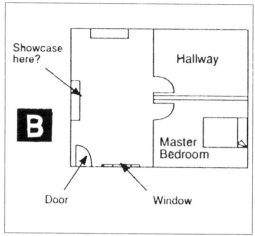

something 'good' like a pond, a river or even a bank, then having the mirror to attract these 'goodies' would be positive.

If you have a T-junction, pole or tree and the direction is not too appropriate, the mirror would attract influences that could cause disharmony in your household.

The painting of a night scene is in the best position possible—after all, the bedroom is where you retire for a good night's sleep.

You may have visitors coming by who comment on the feng shui of your home now and then but remember, they are just amateurs in this line of work.

In the toilet

THERE ARE TWO toilets located on the upper floor of my double-storey house. One is located in the master bedroom, while the other is just outside it.

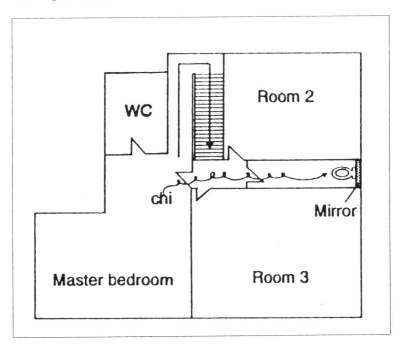

Recently, I changed the toilet tiles and in the common toilet outside the master bedroom, I placed a big mirror facing the door. Can you please tell me if I have put the mirror in the correct position?

Lang
Selangor

MIRRORS ARE INSTRUMENTS that can be used to attract *chi* towards one's direction. So it is not a good idea to place it in a position where it could attract good *chi* from your master bedroom into the toilet, a place where wastes are disposed of.

It is best for you to remove the mirror and place it at the side of the toilet wall.

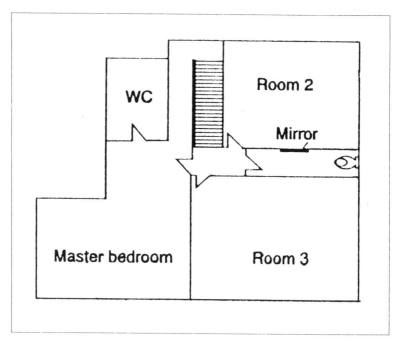

In the bedroom

MY ROOM IS rather small (12'x 10') and the layout is as shown in Plan 1. Since I intend to change the layout to give me more space (as shown on Plan 2), can you please advise?

Is it all right to sleep with one's feet facing the mirror of the dressing-table? If not, can I cover up the mirror with a poster? Please note that my mirror is fixed onto the dressing-table and can't be removed easily.

Alex Chang
Penang

AS YOUR ROOM is only 120 sq. ft. in built-up area, it is rather difficult to squeeze some extra space out of it.

Your Plan 2 would have been fine except for one thing: your bed would be facing the dressing-table with a mirror attached.

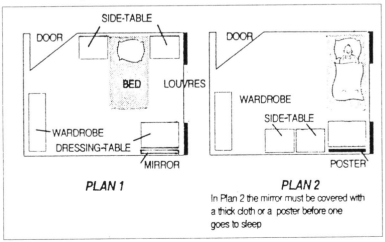

PLAN 1

PLAN 2

In Plan 2 the mirror must be covered with a thick cloth or a poster before one goes to sleep

Since you did mention that it is difficult to remove the mirror, perhaps you could cover it with a piece of cloth or a poster before you go to sleep.

Facing the door

IS THE ARRANGEMENT of furniture in my room in harmony with the forces of nature?

Christina Law
Petaling Jaya

ALLOWING THAT DRESSING-TABLE with the mirror to face the door is helping energy to leak out from your room.

To rectify this negative situation, place your dressing-table between the two beds. The cupboard can be shifted to the spot vacated by the dressing-table while the writing-table can be moved nearer to the door.

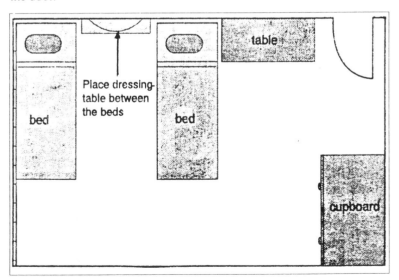

Trouble-making mirror

MY FAMILY AND I moved into a new house last year and since then, I have been suffering from insomnia. I am also having problems with my studies. My room is rather small and there is not much I can do about the furniture's arrangement. What should I do?

Jackie Lai
Kuala Lumpur

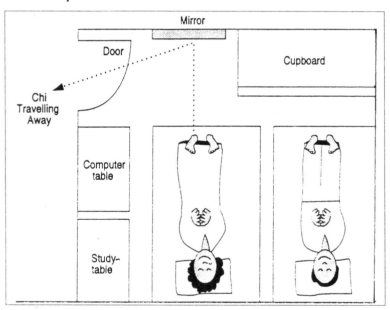

YOUR FURNITURE SHOULD remain as they are. However, the mirror which faces you directly when you are sleeping is causing your *chi* to be siphoned away.

Its effect on your brother is less sever since his image is being blocked by the big cupboard. You should relocate the mirror.

Above the door

I WOULD APPRECIATE it if you could kindly answer these questions:
□ *Will any disadvantage occur if my main door does not face the main gate?*
□ *Will there be any adverse effects if a large monsoon drain runs directly in front of my house?*
□ *What if my house is situated near a busy intersection?*
□ *Does rearing dogs affect one's feng shui?*

Ken

TO HAVE THE main door not facing the gate is in fact a better choice than to have the door and gate directly facing each other. In a straight line, the *chi* travels too fast and will not be good for one's feng shui.

As your house faces a large monsoon drain which flows in a straight line, one could say that money would come your way but one would have a hard time saving up. To reverse that effect place an ordinary mirror on top of your front door so that wealth that passes your house will be attracted into the house.

Your house is also situated next to an intersection. As the tree is planted at the vulnerable point at the edge of your garden where *sha chi* and lights from incoming vehicles can be absorbed, you need not worry.

Lastly, as dogs are known as man's best and faithful friends, rearing them will not hurt your feng shui. However more positive vibes, when brown- or beige-coloured dogs are reared, will enhance your fortune.

Broken mirror

I ACCIDENTALLY DROPPED a mirror which ended up in pieces. Please advise me on what to do.

Chris MLC
Klang

IN THE OLDEN days, the Chinese believed that the mirror which reflects one's image can also imprison a soul. They believe that seven years of bad luck follows a broken mirror. However, recent findings show that this is not necessarily true.

To be on the safe side, however, what you can do is wrap up the broken pieces in a dark piece of cloth and bury it in one corner of your garden. This way, your bad luck is buried.

Doors

The way to good fortune

I READ IN your column that the door which is commonly used to enter the house is considered the main entrance in feng shui. So how would you rate the feng shui of a house where the main entrance is via the garage door?

Dr Jagjit Kaur
Sitiawan

TO SEEK HARMONY in feng shui, a geomancer does not just look at one door. All the doors in the house—including the gate—are important too as they are interrelated.

The main gate which leads to the house is considered the most important entrance. If the main gate is out of harmony with its surroundings, then its tantamount to a bad start. But if the main gate is in harmony with the natural forces, then you can consider the garage door as the second most important door.

The side door of the garage comes next. The main door at the hall which is seldom used can be considered the dormant door.

Wind-chime

WE WOULD APPRECIATE very much if you could give us some general advice on the house-plan enclosed.

Jess & Ben

TO SLOW DOWN the swift flow of *chi* from the main door towards the kitchen, hang a *feng ling* (wind-chime) at the main entrance.

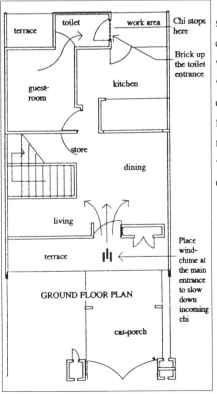

The bathroom is seen as a source of water, and hence is considered a symbol of wealth. By having two doors, wealth will be seen flowing out. Thus, it would be difficult for the occupants to become rich. You can solve this by walling up one of the entrances.

Door sentry

WE HAVE JUST moved into a new house. My wife and I have different opinions on the placing of the family altar.
Coming from a Buddhist family, I do not like the altar to be placed in the dining area. I think it should be placed on the first floor. What is your opinion?

Low Siew Por
Petaling Jaya

IF THE ALTAR is in the dining area, there is a danger that the legs of the diners will be at the same level as the altar, if the altar is lowly positioned. It is disrespectful to have your legs facing the altar.

On the other hand, placing the altar on the first floor would leave your ground floor unprotected. I suggest that you place the altar near the main door to act as a sentry against intruders.

Timber door

I HAVE BEEN staying in my present house for the past six years and everything has gone smoothly so far.

However, I would like to change my main door, which is a sliding glass door with aluminium frame, to that of a solid timber door.

Enclosed is a plan of my house. Please advise.

Jeff
Sibu

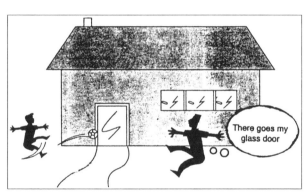

DUE TO ITS transparent nature, a sliding glass door is often known as a "liquid door". *Chi* is believe to be able to travel freely into the house, whether the door is opened or closed. So if you replace it with a timber door, *chi* can enter the house only when the door is open.

In feng shui, houses should use solid doors for their front entrance as this gives the house a well-protected look. At the same time, the flow of *chi* can be easily controlled. The glass door is best suited for offices and business premises where you want lots of *chi* to flow in to bring about lots of business.

Door face door

I READ FROM your column that the front and back doors of a house should not be aligned. If the front and back door of a flat are aligned but separated by a wall, is it all right?

Y.E. Tan
Penang

IN THE PRACTICE of feng shui, a rule of thumb is that doors should not be aligned in any dwelling or office. As *chi* travels or flows in a straight line, it would be lost as soon as it enters the front door by quickly leaving through the back. Thus, other rooms in the house, flat or office would not benefit.

The wall (between the two areas or rooms) would block the *chi* coming into the front room from flowing out immediately through the back room; therefore, the *chi* will circulate around the rest of the house. So a wall separating your front and back doors should be all right.

Slanted door

I HOPE YOU can enlighten me on the following questions:

☐ *Would a badly fitted main door and bathroom door affect the occupants? To be more specific, the height of the doors on one end is lower than the other.*

☐ *What is the significance of reversing a car into the driveway? When I return home from work, I always reverse into the porch as it is convenient to drive out early the next morning.*

☐ *My back neighbour's house is higher than mine. Are there any effects on me?*

K.H. Low
Cheras

IN ANSWER TO your first question, the main door of the house is important as it opens and welcomes fortune into the interior. As for the

ORIGINAL PLAN

SUGGESTED PLAN

bathroom where there is plenty of water, we can also consider it a place where wealth and fortune are stored. Thus, doors with one end lower than the other is out of balance with nature. Therefore, your fortune entering the house can be said to be erratic.

To balance both doors, you can change them to conventional ones. And if that is not possible, then paint a white line across it to halt your fortune and wealth from sliding down.

By reversing your car into the driveway you have to face the front gate or the exit before you get down from the car. This action symbolizes that your heart is outside the house. It would be good to drive your car into the porch when you reach home. This way you really show that you are coming home instead of being ready to go out at any time. This action will be good especially when you are not always at home to spend time with your family. It is also good for your career.

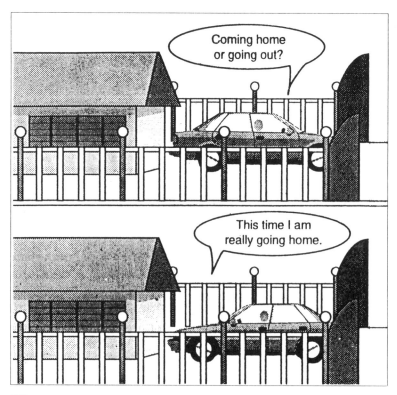

Since the front of your house is not blocked by anything, then there will be no bad effects moving towards your direction. To have the back portion of your neighbour's house higher than yours, you can truly say that the back of your house is being guarded and protected.

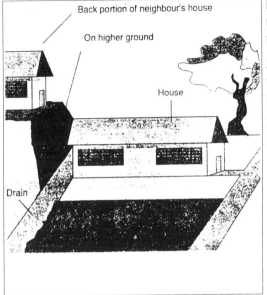

Next to sliding door

I AM GETTING married soon and need your advice on where I should place the bed and built-in cupboard.

To Be Married Soon Batu Caves

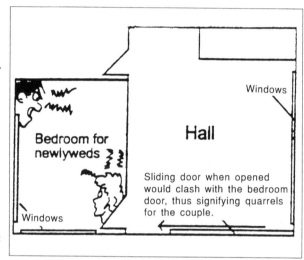

Bedroom for newlyweds

Hall

Windows

Windows

Sliding door when opened would clash with the bedroom door, thus signifying quarrels for the couple.

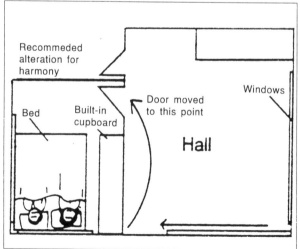

Recommeded alteration for harmony

Bed

Built-in cupboard

Door moved to this point

Windows

Hall

FROM THE PLAN you enclosed, I notice that the bedroom door is very near to the main door of your house. This could spell trouble for your marriage later on as the sliding main door, when opened clashes with the bedroom door.

It is advisable to change the position of the bedroom door and put it at the far-end corner of the room. You can then place the bed towards the wall where the windows are, to give it added support, strength and stability. The built-in cupboard can be placed as shown in the diagram.

Shadowed door

I HAVE A six-year old brother who likes to play with 1, 5 and 10 sen coins by pushing them against each other on my bedroom floor.

I wonder if this causes any side- effects because there are times at night when I wake up suddenly with the feeling that there is some force or presence in the room. This nightmarish occurrence has somehow affected my career. Please advise.

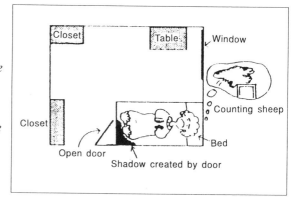

Mum
Petaling Jaya

I REMEMBER THE case of a very rich man who would throw coins over his shoulder, one at a time, whenever he walked. Following close behind would be his maid or servant who would quickly bend down and retrieve them. No one knew why. When the old man passed away, his fortune somehow followed suit—there was nothing left for his heirs. Some people believe it was the act of throwing coins over his shoulder which signified that he was getting rid of his heir's fortune.

I also have a friend who likes to reach into his trouser pocket and jingle the coins there whenever he has a meeting. A psychologist wrote in a book on human behaviour once that whenever someone does that, it is because he is lacking in financial means. And he was right.

Where the supernatural is concerned, however, it is commonly believed that when coins are knocked against each other, the clicking sound reverberates into the spirit dimension, calling such beings forth. Such beliefs are echoed in the use of bells and chimes to summon spirits in a number of rituals found throughout the world.

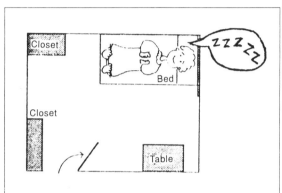

If you want to stop your younger brother from playing with coins, give him some toys to play with instead.

As for your bedroom, it is too near the door and will always fall under the shadow of the door when it is opened. To put your furnishings in better harmony with each other, move the bed to the far wall of the room as shown in the diagram.

Too many doors

MY TERRACED HOUSE has two front doors. One is a wooden door which opens into the driveway. The other is a sliding aluminium door which is located at the front of the house.

For good feng shui, should I use one or both doors?

K.T. Kok
Kuala Lumpur

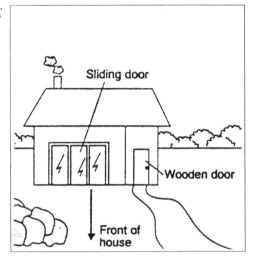

ONE OF THE basic principles of feng shui is that if a house is big, it must have a big door and if a house is small, a small door would be the perfect choice. Since yours is a terraced house, it would be bad feng shui to use both doors as this will cause too much *chi* to flow in.

Perhaps you should just stick to the small

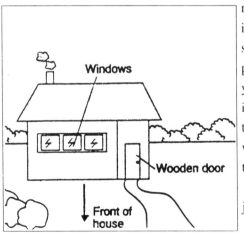

door which leads to the driveway, and keep the sliding door closed. This will help restore balance and harmony all round.

Or, if you like a more permanent solution, you might want to make some renovation and replace the sliding door with a set of windows instead.

Faces staircase

MY FRONT DOOR opens to face the staircase. How does this affect the feng shui of my house?

Chan

FROM THE
DRAWING, it
doesn't appear that
your entrance comes
face to face with the
staircase but the
store-room door
instead.

An easy solution
is to hang a
wind-chime at the
store-room entrance
to break the direct
flow of *chi*.

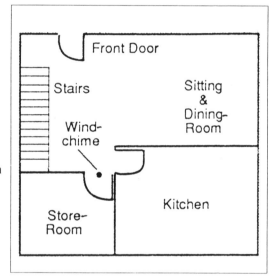

In line with gate and staircase

MY DOUBLE-STOREY HOUSE is on higher ground than that of my neighbour opposite. My house faces the east, and has a hill at the back.

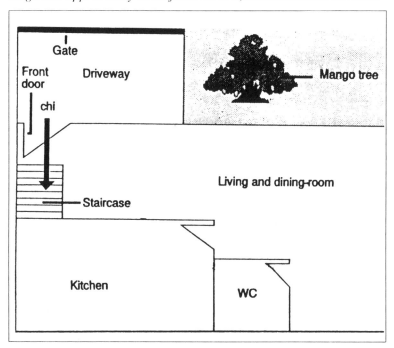

Six years ago I planted a mango tree in the front garden. It has now grown into a big tree.

The main door of my house faces the staircase which leads up stairs. Can you please advice?

Lee

Practical Feng Shui for the Home

YOUR HOUSE WHICH sits on higher ground and faces the east with a hill behind it, enjoys a very good position in terms of feng shui. The mango tree in your garden has no ill bearing towards you and your family.

However, with the direct alignment of your main entrance and staircase, *chi* travels too swiftly into the house. To slow down the motion of that forceful *chi*, you could hang a string of ornamental beads at the front of your staircase.

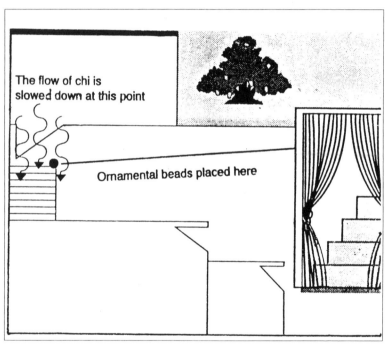

The flow of chi is slowed down at this point

Ornamental beads placed here

Main gate, front door and staircase in alignment

I AM BUYING a double-storey house soon. Can you please tell me whether it is good or bad feng shui if the main gate and the front door faces the staircase?

Lily
Kuala Lumpur

AS ALL *CHI* travelling in a straight line can prove to be too forceful, a gate and a main door which are in line with each other is considered bad feng shui. The same applies when the staircase of the house is aligned with the gate and the main door.

When faced with such a situation, there are two things you can do. A temporary measure would be to place a screen or partition between the staircase and the door, that is, if space allows.

A more permanent measure would be to move the main door elsewhere, thus breaking the straight line of *chi*.

Three in alignment

MY HOUSE, WHICH faces the north sits on higher ground than the row of houses opposite. My sitting-room door is directly aligned to the kitchen door and the back door of the house.

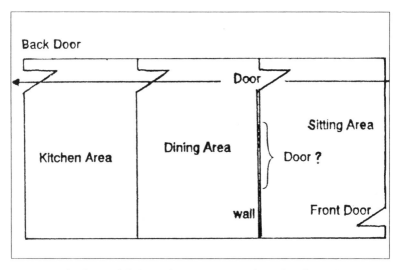

I am thinking of shifting the sitting-room door that faces the front door. Is that a good idea?

Madam S.M. Liew
Ipoh

IT IS GOOD to have your house sited on higher ground than the surrounding houses, but since it faces the north, the good feng shui is somewhat diminished. This negative influence of the north can be averted by placing a *pakua* at your front door.

Another weak point is that your front window is aligned with the sitting-room door, the kitchen door and the back door. As the alignment of doors is too direct, it would cause *chi* to disperse too quickly, thus rendering it difficult for luck and wealth to accumulate. It wouldn't help too, to shift the sitting-room door as suggested.

What you can do to enjoy some brightness and good feng shui is to knock down the wall of the dining area, and have a low shelf to separate the hall from the dining area.

As for the back door, you can shift it to the other end of the kitchen so that it would not overlap each other.

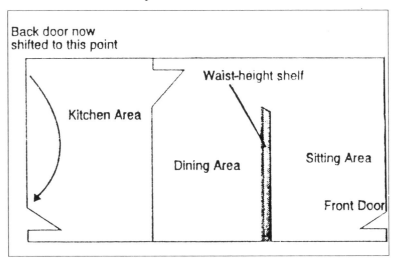

In alignment

WE ARE SHARING a house with my brother-in-law. My husband and I occupy the master bedroom; the door of the room is directly aligned to the back door. Both my husband and his brother are businessmen. Although my husband's business is good, he can hardly save any money whereas his brother can. Can you tell me what is wrong?

ESE
Teluk Intan

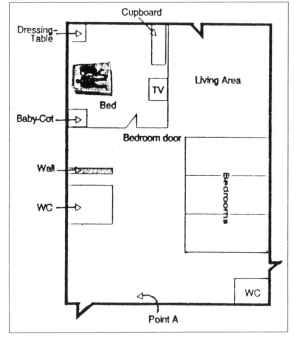

YOUR BED, BEDROOM door and back door are aligned—this is considered bad feng shui. After a hard day's work, you retire to bed only to have part of your wealth siphoned away. I suggest that you change the position of your bed away from the bedroom door. You should shift the back door to the far end as shown in the diagram. Otherwise, hang a long scroll at Point A.

Luck running out

WE BOUGHT A house 12 years ago with our hard-earned money.

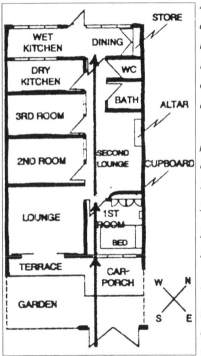

Since then we seemed to be dogged by bad luck as every member of the family suffers from ill health. As far as money is concerned, more goes out than comes in.

Some friends suggested that perhaps the feng shui of the house has brought us bad luck. Enclosed is our house-plan. Can you please advise?

K.S. Cheong
Kuala Lumpur

YOUR HOUSE FACES the south-east which is an auspicious direction. However, it should be noted that the main gate, the window of the first bedroom, its door, and the dinning-hall door all lie in a straight line. So it is no surprise that your family always ends up broke. As *chi* travels too swiftly in a straight line, the health of your family members will be affected too.

You should move your main gate over to the garden. Scale down the size of your sliding door, and have it at one corner of the house, as shown in the diagram. You can fix windows in front for better ventilation and lightning.

With all these renovation, *chi* that enters your house will be better controlled, and can travel more smoothly to benefit the different areas in your house. This will bring about greater harmony and balance into your home.

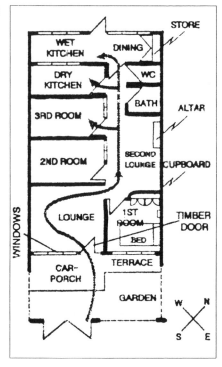

Dotting the knobs

THERE IS A bathroom in my house which is shared by Bedrooms 1 and 2. However, I intend to close the door at Bedroom 2 as I understand that it is bad feng shui for a door to face another door.

Enclosed is a proposed plan of the toilet. Kindly comment.

Mrs Lina Lim
Penang

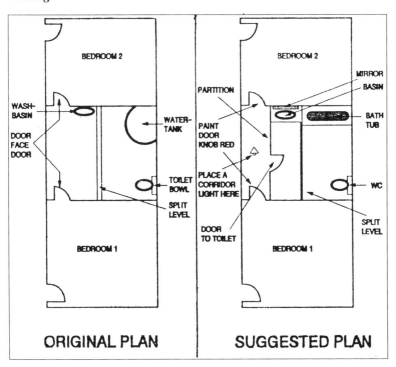

ORIGINAL PLAN   **SUGGESTED PLAN**

YOUR PROPOSED PLAN looks all right, provided your bed is not positioned to face the toilet door and its mirror.

There is another way round the problem though. You can keep the two doors as they are; just paint a red dot in the middle of the door knobs, so that the doors would be 'eyeing' each another to ensure that no quarrel occurs in the family. Erect a partition to form a narrow corridor as shown in the diagram, and open up a common door for the toilet.

Toilet fronting

RECENTLY, I MOVED into a double-storey house. The toilet faces the main entrance. Is this bad feng shui?

And if so, how can I rectify the situation?

Jennifer
Kuala Lumpur

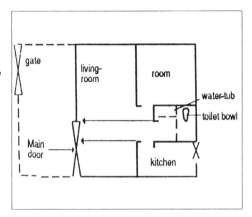

WHEN ENTERING A house, it is the first impression that counts. As the toilet is a place for clearing out waste-matter, it is undesirable to be greeted by such a place upon entering your own home. To improve the situation, you can seal off the toilet entrance and open a door in the spare room instead.

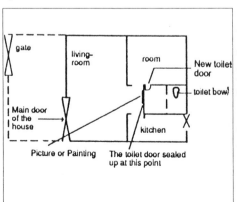

And on the new blank wall that you have just created, you can hang a picture or painting to enhance the look of your living-room and improve the feng shui of your house.

Fortune flowing out

SINCE MOVING INTO this house, we have not had much luck.
Enclosed is an illustration of my house. Opposite is a neighbour's
house which sits on higher ground.

Aries & Virgo
Kuala Lumpur

SINCE YOUR NEIGHBOUR'S house overshadows your house, you
should put a *pakua* in front of your house for better luck.

However, the real
problem lies with the
kitchen sink. As your
sink—which symbolizes a
source of wealth—faces
the main entrance and
back entrance, much of
your fortune is being
siphoned away from both
directions.

I suggest that you
move the sink to a more
enclosed area in the
kitchen.

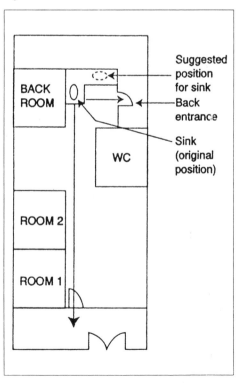

Townhouse:
Where to put the door

MY BROTHER-IN-LAW AND I share a house. He lives upstairs. Car-porch No. 1 is the entrance to his residence while Car-porch No. 2 is mine.

Since Bedroom No. 2 faces the sliding door entrance, I intend to build a wall there instead and have the new entrance lead into the kitchen.

Mrs Theresa Lim
Kuala Lumpur

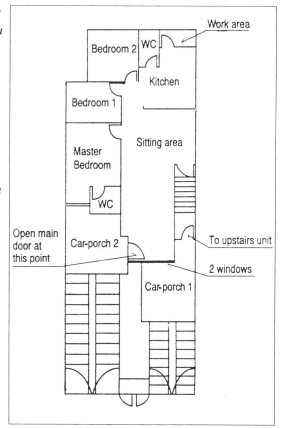

BY HAVING THE new entrance of Bedroom No. 2 leading to the kitchen, it also ends up facing a rubbish container, thus bad luck is in store. However, since such changes would turn out to be worse because cooking fumes may find its way in, it is best that the bedroom door be left as it is.

To offset the bad luck, extend your sitting-room forward and have the main door by the side. As for brightness, have two windows installed as illustrated and have a full-height wall erected so that the rubbish area would not be seen from the inside of the house.

Seeing eye-to-eye

IN MY APARTMENT, the master bedroom faces the two toilets. As for the other two bedrooms, their doors face each other. How do you suggest I improve the feng shui?

Vincent Lim
Kuala Lumpur

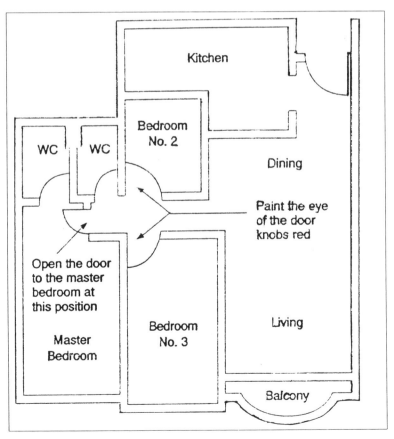

Practical Feng Shui for the Home

HAVING A TOILET facing your master bedroom would allow *sha chi* and bacteria to have easy access to your bedroom and yourself when you sleep. As there are two toilets, *sha chi* would double in your direction.

For a more harmonious situation, brick up the door area and have the entrance placed in an alternative spot (see diagram) so that the door would not face the toilet.

As for the other two bedrooms, paint the eyes of the doorknobs red so that occupants of both rooms would 'see eye-to-eye' and quarrels would be avoided.

PART
22

Bedrooms

Sleeping directions

I HAVE THREE questions; I wonder if you can help me.
- [ ] *Is it all right for a person to sleep with his legs or head facing the door? Does this include main doors or is it just the bedroom door?*
- [ ] *Is it bad luck to hang clothes near the small shrine where I usually pray?*

MJMB
Negeri Sembilan

WHEN SLEEPING, A person should not face the bedroom door because this will drain his vital energy. You need not worry about the main door because the walls in the bedroom acts as a check to the outflow of *chi*.

As a place of worship is considered holy and revered, one should have respect for such a place and not hang clothes there.

Knife-shaped room

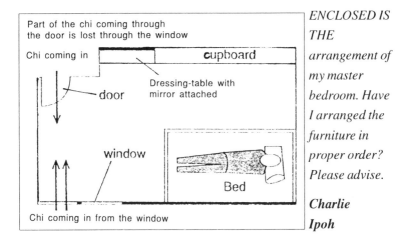

Part of the chi coming through the door is lost through the window

Chi coming in

cupboard

Dressing-table with mirror attached

door

window

Bed

Chi coming in from the window

ENCLOSED IS THE arrangement of my master bedroom. Have I arranged the furniture in proper order? Please advise.

Charlie
Ipoh

FIRSTLY, YOU WILL notice that your room takes on the shape of a knife. By placing your dressing-table at the edge of that knife shape, the mirror will only attract you towards that area when you sleep. Thus you would be 'chopped up' in whatever you do when you position yourself in that vulnerable position.

To create some positive vibes, align

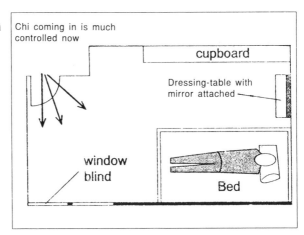

Chi coming in is much controlled now

cupboard

Dressing-table with mirror attached

window blind

Bed

your dressing-table with your bed as shown in the diagram so that the mirror will not do you any harm. As your door faces the windows and the glass windows are transparent, *chi* is able to flow in and out in both directions which may not augur positively for a bedroom.

To control these clash of elements, you may either place window blinds or curtains at these points mentioned in the diagram.

Odd-shaped room

I LIVE IN a single-storey house. But after recent renovations, two of the rooms were taken by other people and I was left with an odd-shaped one.

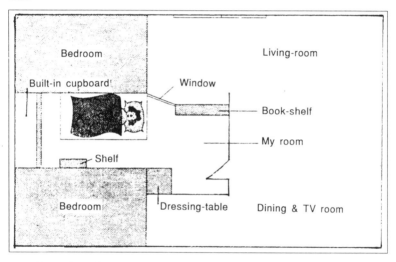

I have been living in this house since 1986 and all this time I have been experiencing bad luck. Now it has got worse in that I have problems with my career and I keep getting into accidents. Please advise.

Leow Mei
Petaling Jaya

TRULY, YOU HAVE a very odd-shaped room. From your illustration, I assume it is so narrow because it was either a store open space in the house before it was converted into a bedroom.

I notice that that part of your room which slants down to an angle to where the windows are, starts at the point where the head of your bed is placed. This is very unbalanced and to live in a room with such a shape can only cause problems in your life.

I suggest you vacate the room and move into another room if you can. Otherwise, I am afraid you will continue to be dogged by bad luck and calamities.

Bed facing door

IN AN EARLIER article you mentioned the importance of the position of the bed. My daughter is staying in a residential hall at an overseas university. The bed in the room she occupies faces the door which I hear is not a good position. But the room is small and she cannot move the bed around. She cannot ask for a change of room because these have all been allocated.

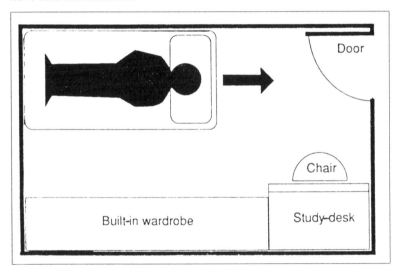

Besides, the furniture in some of the other rooms are also arranged the same way. There is a built-in wardrobe on one side of the room as well as a study-desk with a book-rack fixed to the wall and a light, so there is no way the bed can be moved around. My daughter sleeps with her head near the door. The bed does not have a headboard.

Madam S.L. Cheng
Petaling Jaya

MADAM CHENG, IT is commonly held that we should not sleep with our feet pointing towards a door. Neither should we sleep with the head facing the door either.

To solve this problem, tell your daughter to put up a partition (a folding screen, perhaps) at the foot of the bed.

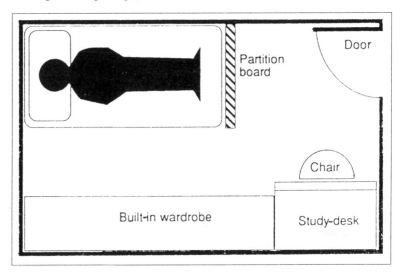

Sleeping on the floor

*I AM A student who will be sitting for my examinations soon. Please
tell me what you think of my bedroom. I usually do not sleep on the bed
but on the floor. How can I enhance my room's feng shui?*

Vincent Lee
Kuala Lumpur

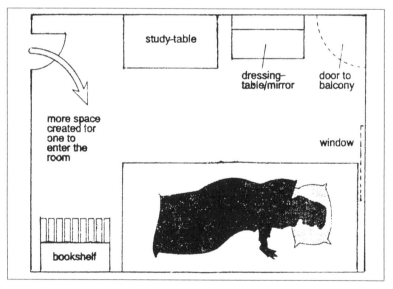

IT DOES NOT matter whether you sleep on the floor so long as you see
that you are protected from the yin *chi* which emanates from the floor.

Your room is rather small but do not worry, it can still be arranged
to meet the requirements of feng shui.

Place the head of your bed near the window and shift your bookshelf to the foot of the bed. The dressing-table can be placed next to the
study-table. That way you'll have more space to move around.

Bed behind door

COULD YOU HELP me to arrange my bedroom furniture to bring about better feng shui?

Jenny Tan
Kuala Lumpur

IT IS NOT ideal to have your bed behind a door. It would be better to have your bed at the centre of the room.

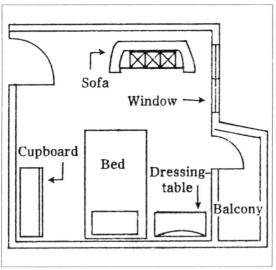

As for the bathroom which is at one corner of the bedroom, having the dressing-table/ mirror close to it is more convenient. You can have your cupboard at the other end of the room.

Toys

EVER SINCE MY parents rearranged the furniture in my room, I find that I cannot concentrate on my studies.

I also came across one of your articles which states that books are best not kept under the bed. How about toys? Please advise.

Study Problem
Melaka

YOUR ROOM SEEMS rather cramped. As you did not mention anyone else using your room, I assume you have the double-bed all to yourself. Removing the double-bed will create more space in your room.

As for the cupboard that is found near the door, it can be placed nearer to your bed as illustrated in the diagram.

On the question of whether the toys under your bed would have an effect on you, I would advise that you keep the bottom of the bed clean.

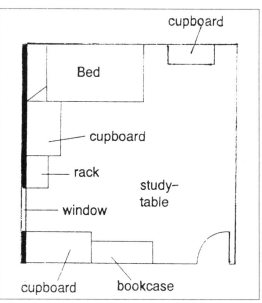

Double-decker

I AM GOING to double deck the two beds in my room. Please help me rearrange the furniture so that I will have good feng shui.

Laureen
Kuala Lumpur

THE BEST PLACE for you to double deck the bed is near the window. Place the book-rack where the table now is so that it will be easier for you to move. The table can be shifted to the book-rack's slot.

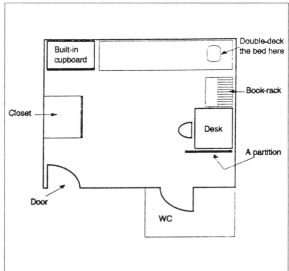

Place a partition between your beds and the water-closet so that you will not have to look at it directly when you go to sleep.

Centre placing

I AM GETTING
married soon.
Please advise on
the placing of the
bedroom furniture.
I am thinking
of placing the bed
on the left side of
the room, with our
feet towards the
window and the
dressing-table and cupboard in between the two windows.

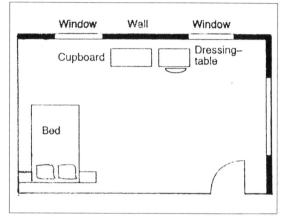

James Lee
Alor Setar

IF YOU SLEEP
facing the window,
you may find the
street-lights
streaming towards
your face. Since
your room is rather
long, you should
place your bed in a
central position
between the two
windows. Thus the

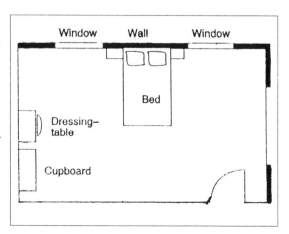

stream of light coming into your bed will be balanced on the right and left of your bed, to make your marriage a success. Place the cupboard and dressing-table on the other side of the wall.

Sun on your back

*I HAVE BEEN living in this house for the past eight years, but I don't
seem to be making any progress financially. In fact, things are getting
from bad to worse. I am all right healthwise and so are my studies.*

*Enclosed is a plan showing the furniture arrangements in my
room. Please advise.*

Mohana
Klang

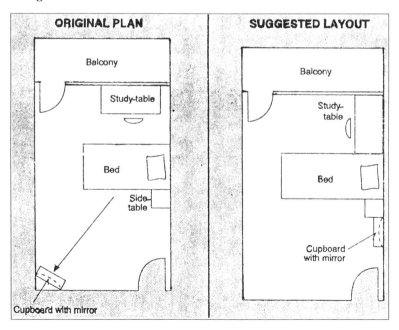

ACCORDING TO THE plan you enclosed, the morning sun rises from
the back of your house from the far right. Thus the sun would set in the
far left, making your front room too hot in the evenings. This may

prove uncomfortable for studying or relaxation at that time of the day. You could install a ceiling fan to cool the room.

Regarding the arrangement, place your study-table towards the wall so that the rays from the evening sun will fall from behind you and will not shine into your eyes.

The mirror attached to the cupboard will reflect your image when you are in bed, leaving you wakeful and restless. Reposition it near the door as shown in the diagram.

Shoe-shaped room

MY BEDROOM DOOR faces the kitchen door. To prevent loss of chi from my room, I have put up a curtain. An I doing the right thing?

Mrs A.S. Wong
Kuala Lumpur

YOUR SKETCH SHOWS that you have a shoe-shaped room. Its weakest point is the heel which is where the windows are. You have prevented yourself from being 'stamped' on, by placing your bed in a good position. So, your sleep is not disturbed. And yes, you have done the right thing by putting up the curtain.

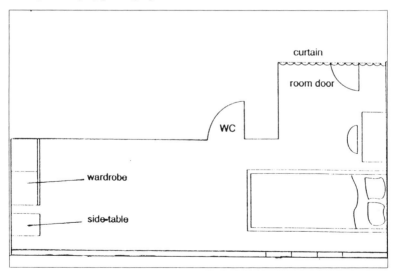

Door opened half-way

FOR MANY YEARS I have been living in this small room during which I have always felt very unhappy. I also find myself in a lot of trouble. For instance, whenever I have saved up some money, I would suddenly get tempted to buy some unnecessary expensive things.

Then in the middle of last year, I lost my job and I have not been able to find another suitable job since. Could all this have something to do with bad feng shui in my room? Will rearranging my furniture help?

Frankie Foo
Sabah

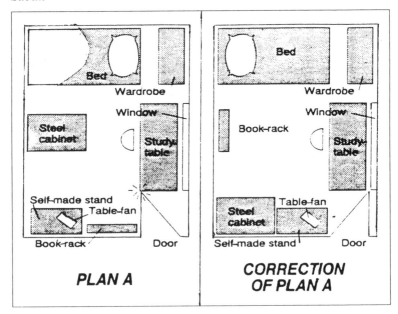

PLAN A

CORRECTION OF PLAN A

I HAVE MENTIONED before that the head must always be positioned against a wall of the room for stability. But your bed is the reverse; so you must turn it around. How you place your furniture in relation to your room door is also important because they effect the flow of *chi*.

Your study-table is too close and partially blocks the door opening and this can only cause imbalance and bad luck. You should therefore push your table further inside your room so that the door can be fully opened.

The steel cabinet is also too close to your bed. You should place it in the corner of the room and rearrange your book-rack and the self-made stand according to the recommended layout.

Ill wind at night

MY ROOM IS rather small and whenever I try to study, my concentration lapses. Could this be the cause of bad feng shui?

**Ng Eng Ho
Selangor**

THE PRESENT POSITION of your bed shows that *sha chi* coming from the toilet will be directed towards your face. It is not a good idea to place to towel-rack near the window next to your bed. The wind will carry the smell of soiled items back to you.

For better harmony, place your bed next to the window, and your study-table towards the wall as shown in the illustration.

The towel-rack can be placed near the toilet, while the book-rack would better complement your need if placed at the foot of the bed so that it faces the study-table.

The rearrangement of furniture is restricted by the size of your room. You might like to close the door to cut off any distraction when you are studying.

Backbone

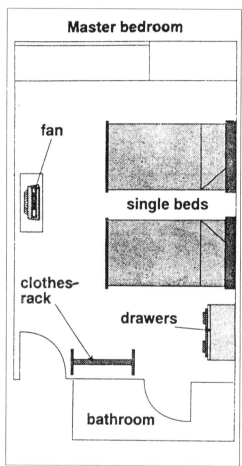

Master bedroom

fan

single beds

clothes-rack

drawers

bathroom

ENCLOSED IS A sketch of my master bedroom. I intend to replace the double-bed with two single-beds and would like your advise on how to position them.

Mrs Ku
Kuala Lumpur

THE TWO SINGLE-BEDS can be placed against the wall to form a backbone. The fan should be positioned at the foot of your beds. Remove the unused TV set to create more space in the room. Place your drawers where the TV set used to be. The clothes-rack should be placed next to the bathroom.

A small room

MY MASTER BEDROOM is very small. Have I arranged my furniture in good order? Please advise.

Linda Yong
Sarawak

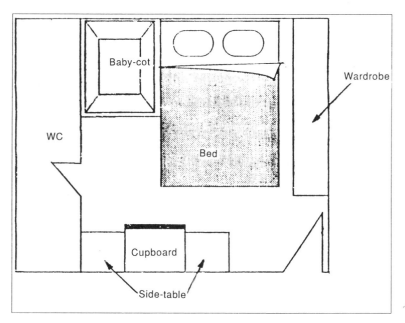

EVEN THOUGH YOUR bedroom may be small, it does not really stop you from creating a healthy environment to live in. For instance, you can turn your sleeping position around by placing your head near the window instead of your legs. As for the baby-cot, it can be placed opposite from where it stands now so that the baby would not have to face the door indirectly, as this would siphon off one's *chi*.

The wardrobe can be placed where the cot was formally. And the cupboard can be sandwiched between the two side-tables as shown in the diagram above.

Space constraints

WE ARE GOING to shift into our new house very soon. My grand-mother is very particular about the position of the beds. I have thought of arranging my two beds as shown in the sketch. Are they in harmony with feng shui?

Ping Ping
Kuala Lumpur

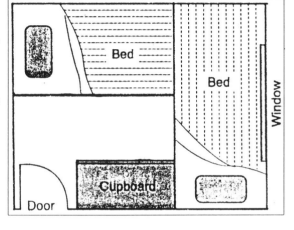

CONSIDERING THE SPACE constraint, the positions you have chosen are the best. Make sure the beds do not face the bedroom door.

Cutting-edge door

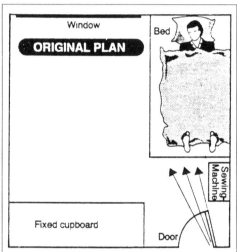

MY ROOM HAS a bed, a sewing machine and a built-in cupboard. I plan to get a study-table and a book-rack. Can you suggest a better arrangement for my furniture?

Audrey Lim
Kuala Lumpur

YOUR PRESENT ARRANGEMENT is not a very good one. Unless the door can be fully opened, it will act as a cutting edge towards your bed direction. This is bad feng shui. Neither is it good to have your feet facing the door when you retire for the night.

I suggest you place your bed on the other side of the room, with the study-table next to it. As

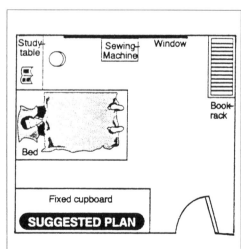

for the sewing machine and the book-rack, they can be easily tucked away into the other corner of the room as shown in the diagram.

With this new arrangement, even though you have two extra pieces of furniture in your room, the area near the entrance looks more spacious and allows for an easy flow of *chi* into your room.

Faces toilet

MY HOUSE FACES south. The master bedroom door faces the bathroom door, which is situated just outside the room.

My husband's health has not been good for some time. To look after him, my daughter and I have been sleeping on the floor next to his bed. I understand that when sleeping you should not have your legs facing the bedroom door. So my daughter and I sleep with our heads facing the door instead.

Please advise us on this matter.

Anxiety
Penang

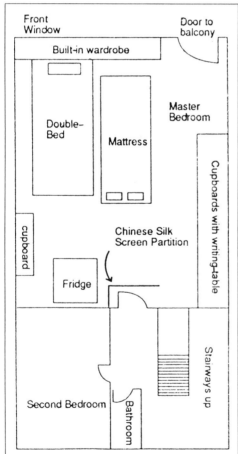

IT IS COMMONLY held that, while it is unwise to sleep with your legs facing the door, it is just as bad to have your head pointed in that direction too.

The easiest solution to this problem, judging from the diagram you provided, is to place a Chinese silk screen across the doorway as shown.

Also, take note that when you and your daughter sleep on the floor, the mattress should be quite thick. Otherwise, you may suffer from rheumatism later on in life. It is said to be caused by the absorption of too much yin, or "Earth *chi*" into your body.

Toilet in bedroom

CAN YOU PLEASE tell me whether it is good to have my bedroom facing the toilet door? I seem to fall sick all the time, and my father is worried that it could be due to the poor feng shui of my room. What do you think?

Leow Wei Shin
Petaling Jaya

YOUR DAD IS right. In feng shui, a door should not face another door because *chi* travels in a straight line, and it would move through the doors too swiftly without benefiting other parts of the house.

In your case, since your bedroom door faces the toilet, the bad *chi* from the toilet could be affecting your health. You can rectify the situation easily by relocating the toilet door.

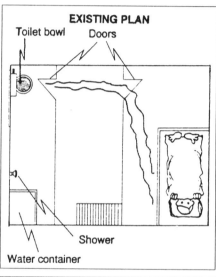

EXISTING PLAN

Toilet bowl   Doors

Shower

Water container

NEW PLAN

Sliding door

Bed facing toilet

ENCLOSED IS THE layout of my master bedroom. How do you suggest I rearrange the furniture for better feng shui? The double-bed cannot be moved, however, because it is quite large.

I would like to know if it is all right for my children to study with a bookshelf behind them.

K.H. Wong
Taiping

YOUR MASTER BEDROOM is rather small for any rearrangement. However, having your bed facing the toilet door is not good feng shui.

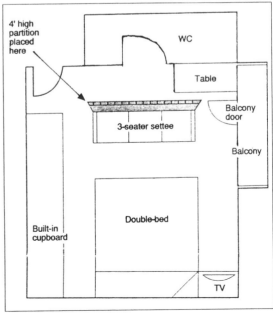

You can still lessen the *sha chi* coming from the toilet by placing a four-foot wooden partition behind your settee and by closing the toilet door.

Having the bookshelf behind your children will not affect their studies. In fact, it symbolizes them being backed by knowledge.

Faces staircase

MY BEDROOM DOOR faces the staircase. The bed and furniture in the room are arranged as shown in the diagram.

How can I improve the harmony of my room?

Steven Tay

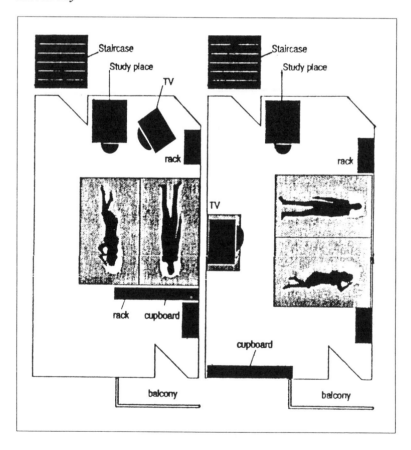

IT IS CONSIDERED lucky to have your room door facing a staircase which leads upwards as it promotes one's position in society.

However, it is not a good idea to sleep with your head or feet facing the door. It is best to change the position of your bed.

As for the cupboard, you can place it at one corner of the room, while the TV can be placed on top of one of the racks as shown in the diagram.

Cupboard blocking

ENCLOSED IS A plan of my bedroom and the furniture arrangement.
Can you please help me to rearrange the furniture if they are not in harmony with the feng shui of the room?

Curious Boney Raub

AS THE CUPBOARD is placed between your bed and the window, it blocks the flow of *chi* towards your resting place. So you are receiving only half the benefit of the incoming *chi*.

You can easily move your bed towards the window, and place your cupboard at the

foot of the bed. By doing so, your bed will be well supported by the wall, which offers solid backing in terms of feng shui. There will be

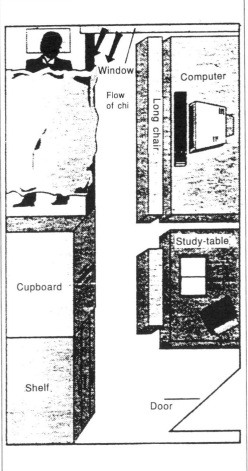

better circulation of *chi* in the room which will enable you to enjoy better health.

Axe in the room

ENCLOSED IS A plan of my bedroom layout. Please advised if the furniture is properly arranged.

C. Dave
Seremban

BY SLEEPING IN The present position, your legs are facing the L-shaped table which symbolizes an axe. This would undermine your success in life. To offset this, rearrange the bed so that it is placed against the wall. Your legs would then face the handle of the axe to give you control of your life.

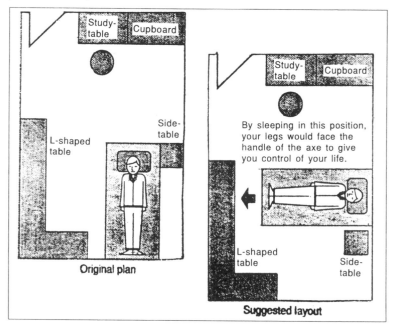

Watch the flow of *chi*

I BOUGHT A dressing-table recently and had our bedroom furniture rearranged. Since then, my husband finds it hard to sleep especially at night. Could this problem have anything to do with the arrangement of the furniture?

Mrs T.C.
Kuala Lumpur

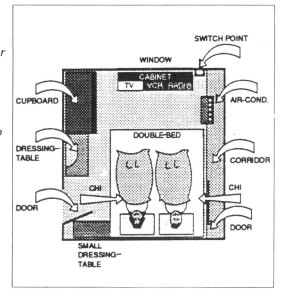

THE ARRANGEMENT OF your room has a lot to do with your bad feng shui, especially when it comes to sleeping. First, the door into the room cannot be fully opened because the dressing-table is in the way. Remember that a door is still a gateway for *chi* whether or not you use it. And because *chi* travels in a straight line, someone lying down in its path would find it hard to sleep.

With so much furniture in it, your room is too cramped for *chi* to circulate properly. To restore the harmony in your room, you can place your bed at the centre of the opposite wall with the big dressing-table next to it. The plug points can be relocated closer to the air-conditioner.

Your cupboard can be moved from the opposite wall to cover the door that leads out into the corridor. Since space is rather limited in your room, you may have to give up the cabinet and use a low table for the VCR and TV. The radio can easily be placed on the cupboard.

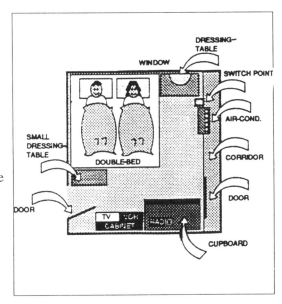

Room have to breathe

ENCLOSED IS A diagram of my bedroom. Could you give me some suggestions on how to place my furniture?

Jonathan
Miri

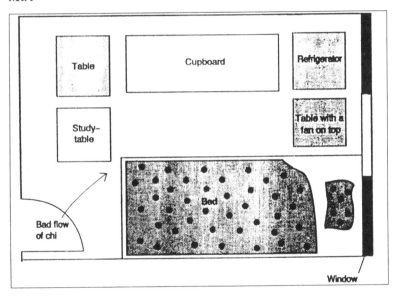

YOUR APARTMENT IS overcramped. Remove the refrigerator and the table with the fan so that you will have more breathing space. Your bed can then be shifted to the far side of your room so that you do not have to sleep with your feet towards the door anymore.

Your refrigerator can be placed at the foot of the bed so that its door ends up facing you to stimulate the inflow of wealth. The cupboard and the writing-table can be placed opposite the side of the bed.

Birds near bedroom window

IS THE FURNITURE arrangement in my room all right? There are also a lot of birds resting above my window. Do their presence affect my wealth and luck?

CW
Petaling Jaya

TO CREATE A more harmonious living environment, place your tables against the wall and move your cupboard away from the entrance to prevent accidents.

As for the birds resting near your window, consider yourself lucky because birds emit a positive aura. However, make sure you clean the compound because bird droppings attract ants.

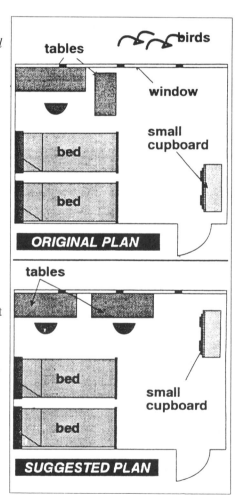

Correct way to sleep

JANET WONG OF Selangor has been having trouble sleeping at night. Writing in response to an earlier article which dealt with sleeping positions, she has enclosed two sketches and wants to know which is preferable.

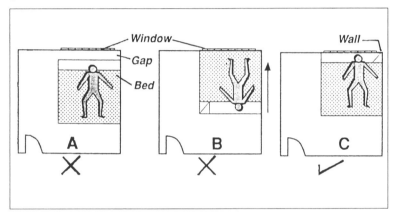

The bed in the first sketch is positioned better than in the second. However, the headboard should be placed firmly against the wall.

If you leave a gap between the headboard and the wall, you may still have a troubled sleep as it can be said that you will have trouble finding 'proper rest'.

The other plan, where one sleeps with the feet pointing the windows, is not advisable. It is best to follow your first plan with a little alteration, that is, placing the headboard of the bed firmly against the wall.

Coffin position

DO YOU TAKE into account comfort, health and safety when you give advice on feng shui positions? I think it is unwise for anyone to place his bed directly below the window. When it rains, water would get in and wet the bed.

My mother is a big fan of yours. She takes your advice very seriously. She now insists that my bed, which faces the door is in a bad position.

I am in the process of buying new furniture. Please tell me the best way to position my bedroom furniture. My mother is driving me nuts.

Katherine Lim
Petaling Jaya

YOU ARE SLEEPING in the "coffin position". Corpses are usually placed in such an alignment before they are buried or cremated the next day. Life-force, or *chi*, leaks out of the physical body which is in such a position.

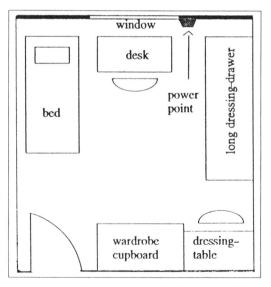

To sleep better, place your bed at the opposite end of the room. The air-conditioner and power points should be positioned in the indicated

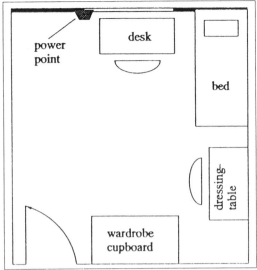

areas. It is all right to place one's bed under the window because most roofs usually extend far enough to keep rain-water away from the windows.

One can always put up an awning if the roof does not provide the necessary protection.

Sharp edge of axe

I AM A 21-year old bank clerk. I have run into lots of bad luck ever since I move into a rented room with a friend two years ago. I am also being sexually harassed by a colleague. My room-mate, on the other hand, is happy and seems to be having all the luck.

Does the feng shui of my room have something to do with my problems?

WLW
Petaling Jaya

YOUR ROOM-MATE'S LEGS face the wall when she is sleeping. The wall serves as a solid foundation and this works to her advantage.

Besides, when the two beds are placed together, an axe shape is formed and unfortunately your sleeping position represents the sharp edge of the axe. In feng shui, this is a vulnerable position and is symbolic of being placed on the chopping board.

To remedy the situation, rearrange the two beds so that the heads of the beds rest against the wall for proper support.

Lastly, place the table near the door and clear away the old newspapers to avoid clutter.

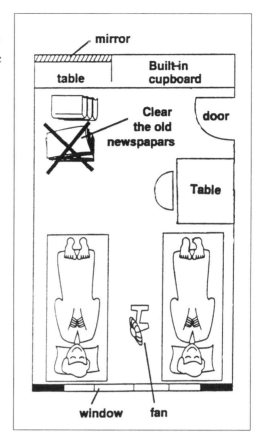

399

Basket case

MY WIFE AND I moved into this flat recently and since then, we have been unlucky. Everyone in my company received a raise or promotion but not me although I have worked very hard. The same goes for my wife. My luck at buying lottery is just as bad.

I wonder if our furniture arrangement has anything to do with our misfortune.

Wong Chin Poh
Penang

THE WASTE-PAPER BASKET in your bedroom is almost in line with your head position when you sleep.

The waste-paper basket is a container for rubbish. To place it parallel to one's head is to associate oneself with useless things. To reverse the effect, place the basket at the foot of your bed.

The other thing you should look into is the mirror which is facing the bed. The mirror is reflecting *chi* from your body and diverting it out through the doorway. You should remove the mirror and place it on the opposite wall.

Your bedroom door faces the main entrance. This also means a loss of *chi* from the bedroom. Install a wind-chime to stem the flow.

Next to kitchen

WE ARE A young married couple, renting a back room next to the kitchen. We have been staying here for the past three years and now we share it with our month-old daughter.

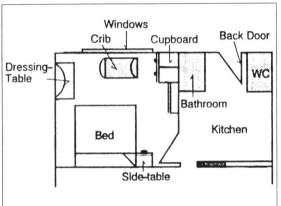

Since moving into this room my husband and I often have heated arguments. I wonder if having our room too near the kitchen has anything to do with it. If so, can you tell me how I can improve things and find peace within my family?

Cal
Melaka

A BEDROOM WHICH is too close to the kitchen is bad feng shui. As the kitchen is a place where food is prepared and cooked, it symbolizes the Fire Element. And because of this fiery element, heated quarrels are likely to occur.

So you should move to a different room. It may take some time for you to find a new room, but meanwhile, to negate the fiery effects, you could paint the walls of your room light green. As green colour gives a cooling effect, this will help to keep tension down and restore some peace in your family.

It would help too, to reposition your bed away from the bedroom door .

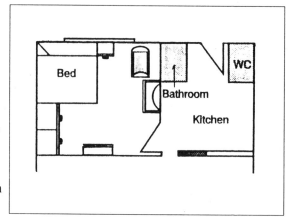

Of colours and beds

MY FAMILY HAS been having a lot of problems since we moved into this terraced house. Could this be caused by bad feng shui? The fence, the gate and the walls in the porch are painted orange and grey. You mentioned in previous articles that a bed backed up by a wall would enhance the feng shui. But most of our beds are placed in different directions. What do you suggest? Is it good feng shui to have the clothes-lines next to our shrine?

Miss Ng
Negeri Sembilan

HAVING ODD COLOURS in one's home reflect one's personality. You may want to change this image by painting your fence silver, with the gate and the porch walls in neutral white. The protruding wall next to the gate is pointing towards your house entrance. As this prevents *chi*

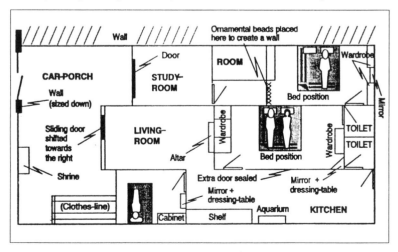

from entering, have this wall sized down and shift your main entrance towards the right as shown in the diagram.

For the master bedroom, have only one door to prevent *chi* from seeping out unnecessarily. As for the bed, it could be backed up against the wall.

In the second room which is shaped like a knife, you may place ornamental hanging-beads to create a more desirable shape. The bed can also be backed up against the wall.

As for the clothes-lines, have the metal bar placed further inside, away from the shrine.

Dead man's shadow

I WILL BE moving into the company lodgings soon. The previous manager lived in the first room but died in the second.

I would like to turn the first room into a guest-room and use the second to store things. I will stay in the third room. Am I making the right choice? Is it all right also to use the dining-table, chairs and cooking utensils left by my late predecessor?

Wendy Gooi
Kuala Lumpur

I UNDERSTAND YOUR fear of the deceased's legacy. Bear in mind that if the late manager had been an upright and sincere person, you have nothing to fear. But if you are uncertain of his character, your own doubt may well spook you psychologically and you may want to 'clean up' the area. A clean-up is used to get rid of a person's bad vibes.

Salt, which is regarded the essence of life, should be dissolved in a cup of water and sprinkled in the premises. It will dissolve old energies and neutralize the place. Then, use incense to cleanse the air and fumigate the ether.

Disturbed by spooks

I SLEEP ON the lower bunk of a double-decker bed. I have experienced bei quai chak (being crushed by spooks) several times. My friend in the upper bunk has never had such disturbances.

Curious
Seremban

TRY SLEEPING THE other way around so that the window and lights are behind your head. This will give you an edge in feng shui.

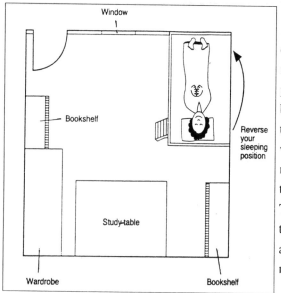

There are many reasons why one is the target of negative forces. A person who is born at a 'weak' time will have a weak aura. This makes him prone to such attacks. The same applies to a person who is a physical or mental weakling.

To boost your aura, make sure you have both physical and mental exercise. Reading is a good mental exercise. In the meantime, there are several tentative ways in which you can protect yourself from disturbances.

If you are a religious person, call on your god to help you. If you do not have a religion, form a mental picture of a white or blue light shielding your body when you sleep.

Bei quai chak

RECENTLY, I EXPERIENCED a severe spell of bei quai chak with a frequency of one or two attacks per week. Although I am not exactly terrified, I find such attacks a source of annoyance and distraction. Could the feng shui of my house be the likely cause of these attacks?

A.K. Lim
Kuala Lumpur

THERE IS NO research to show why some people get *bei quai chak* attacks while others never do. But there are reasons to believe that some people are more susceptible to such attacks as they were born during a weak time of birth, thus rendering them with a weak shield or aura to protect them physically, mentally or spiritually.

To avoid such attacks, you could place a *pakua* at your window. As your balcony door faces your bedroom door, this could allow for quick flow of *chi* and spirit. You can control this by placing a pagoda wind-chime at the balcony door. As for your bed, place the headboard next to the wall to give you a good night's sleep.

If you have done all that is suggested and you still suffer from these attacks, then you could place a sharp knife underneath your bed as spirits are afraid of sharp instruments.

However, if you have children at home, caution should be taken to avoid any accidents.

In happier mood

I AM RENTING a fully furnished room with a girl-friend. Since moving in, I find myself easily irritated, depressed and view life from a gloomy perspective.

Most of the furniture in the room are of bluish and grey tones. Is the furnishing arrangement and colour affecting me somehow?

Curious
Kuala Lumpur

HALF OF ONE bed is under the overhead cabinet. Because of the ill balance of *chi*, a state of depression comes naturally. To offset depression and restore the balance of *chi*, attach a round mirror under the overhead cabinet.

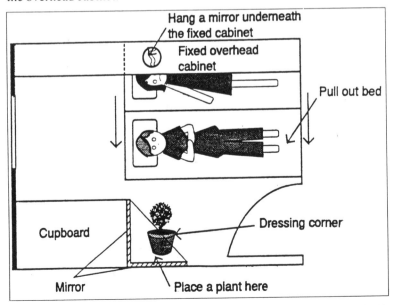

As the mirror symbolizes the Fire Element, having two in your dressing-corner (in a triangle which forms a fire shape) makes your room overheated with tension. To release heat, dismantle the two mirrors and place a plant in the dressing-corner.

The colours grey and blue contribute to the depressive mood. Try to paint your room with bright shades like pink, apple green or neutral white. However, if your landlord does not approve, have lots of nice and bright pictures or paintings on the wall.

L-shaped table

I HAVE BEEN suffering from insomnia since I got married. I wonder if it has anything to do with my bedroom.

Sophia Wong
Port Dickson

IN YOUR PRESENT sleeping position, the L-shaped table which symbolizes an axe seems to knock towards the direction of your head. You can place two bamboo flutes criss-crossed by the side of the table to halt the flow of chopping *chi* from the L-shaped table.

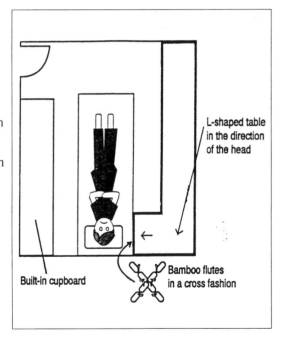

L-shaped table
in the direction
of the head

Built-in cupboard

Bamboo flutes
in a cross fashion

From the Coffin Position

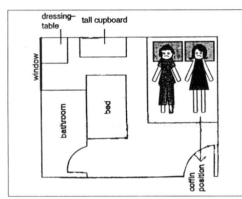

IN MY BEDROOM, the bathroom takes up one-third of the room space and I find that I cannot place my double-bed away from the main door, thus I cannot avoid the Coffin Position.

Can I sleep with my head facing the bedroom door instead?

Housewife
Petaling Jaya

TO REVERSE YOUR position and sleep with your head facing the door would drain your vitality. Since there is no space left to change position of your bed, place a cupboard at the foot of the bed so that it can help prevent *chi* from flowing from your body via the door.

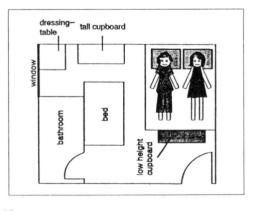

Sleep dogged by nightmare

MY HUSBAND AND I moved into our current house two years ago. Since then we hardly get a peaceful night's sleep. We seem to be having dreams the whole night through. Is there anything wrong with our room?

Mrs Y.K. Cheong
Kuantan

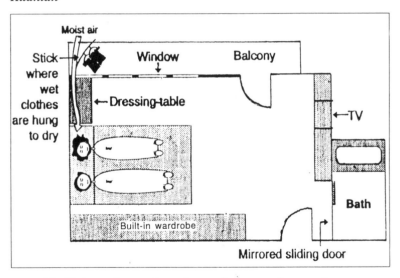

ALL OF US dream in our sleep. Some of us remember our dreams vividly, while others find it hard to recall what they dreamt the night before. However, when we have frequent nightmares, then we are in trouble. This is because a person who does not get a good night's sleep can be certain of waking up to a bad day.

In your case, you might want to place a cover over your TV screen and mirrored door before you retire for the night. Make sure that your cover is not transparent as your *chi* can again be attracted out of the door, thus leaving you without a good night's sleep.

Note too that wet clothing hanging in the balcony may cause the wind to blow the damp air inside, causing you discomfort. Try drying your clothes elsewhere.

However, if your dreams persist, there is a traditional belief that placing a sieve near the top of your head will 'filter' out all your nightmares.

'Sliced' by the door

I HAVE NOT had any luck since moving into my old family house five years ago. I share a room with my brother.

Does the room I am staying in have anything to do with my poor luck?

Seow HK
Penang

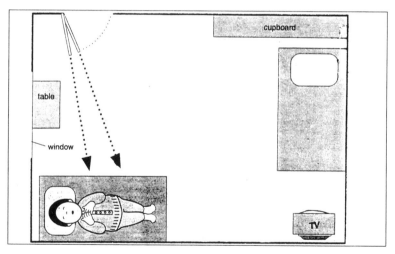

IN TERMS OF feng shui, your room arrangement is not practical as your bed is sliced by the door each time it its opened. This way, it is like one's luck being cut in half.

For better harmony, place your small table and your bed next to your brother's bed. Your new bed position will also let you watch the TV better. A good position for the cupboard is behind the door, but since it will block the window there, place it as illustrated in the diagram.

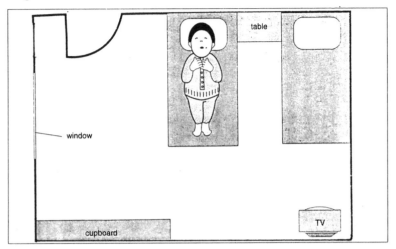

No way out

I READ THAT one's sleeping position should not end up facing the toilet entrance. I have tried to rearrange my bed to face the wardrobe. But I found it impractical because the TV/VCR/hi-fi sets would be out of place.

Is it all right to revert to the old position, because space is very limited in our room?

Madam Lim
Petaling Jaya

LOOKS LIKE YOU cannnot move your furniture around much due to space constraint. However, you can control some of the bad *chi* coming towards your direction when

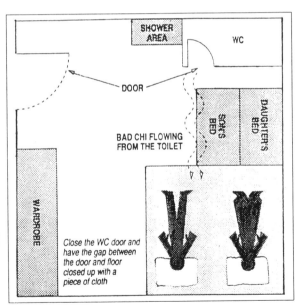

you are asleep: just keep the toilet door closed, and place a piece of cloth in between the door and the floor.

PART
23

Study Areas

Affected by edge of wall

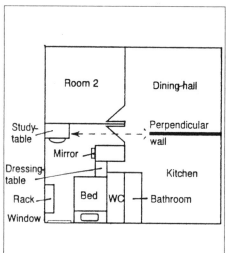

I AM A STUDENT who finds that my studies have been affected since moving into my aunty's house in Klang about 10 months ago.

Could this have something to do with the room I am staying in?

I have enclosed my room layout for your reference.

Aileen Ng
Klang

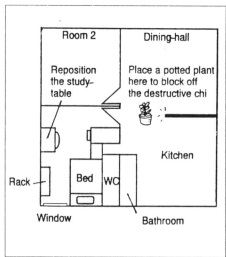

I NOTICE A perpendicular wall in the dining-hall which cuts into the side of your study-table, when your room door is open.

You can rectify the situation by placing a potted plant next to the edge of the perpendicular wall to deflect the *sha chi* coming from the cutting edge.

Alternatively, you can shift the study-table away from the door and place it in the middle of the room as shown in the diagram.

Cannot concentrate

I AM A Form Four student and my luck seems to be running low this year. I think it could be due to the arrangement of my bedroom.

I would be grateful if you could help me rearrange my room according to feng shui so that I can concentrate on my studies.

Sininen Hetki
Johor

TO HAVE YOUR bed facing the door is bad luck. Moreover, the passage between the bed and the bookshelves is too narrow for you to walk through.

To find proper balance, place your bed under the window so that you can enjoy fresh air when you sleep. Place the cupboard with the cutlery and china in the area vacated by the bed.

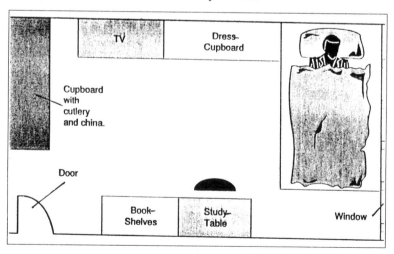

Mirror problem

I WILL BE sitting for my exams soon. Lately, my studies have been affected. Enclosed is my room layout. Kindly advise.

Francis Lee
Penang

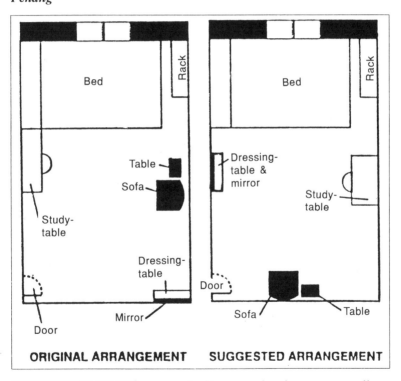

ORIGINAL ARRANGEMENT   **SUGGESTED ARRANGEMENT**

THE MIRROR THAT faces your bed has some bearing on your well-being when you are asleep. To off-set this, move your dressing-table to where your study-table is, and shift your study-table to where the sofa is. As for the sofa, place it in the area as shown in diagram.

Apple green

I AM EASILY tired and lazy to do my studies this year. My grades are starting to slip. My friends who used to lend me an ear are also seemed to be bored with me.

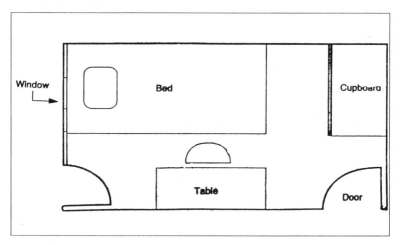

I recall that my mother asked me to rearrange my bedroom last year. It looks like bad luck has been dogging me ever since I have done so. My temper is getting worse and I have been quarrelling with my parents very often.

Is my bedroom arrangement really having a bad effect on me? I sleep on the floor with my feet facing the door.

Bad Luck Charm
Sungai Petani

IT IS VERY bad feng shui to have your back towards the door when you sit down at the study-table. Whenever the door is opened the flow of *chi* is disrupted and this interferes with the concentration of your mind.

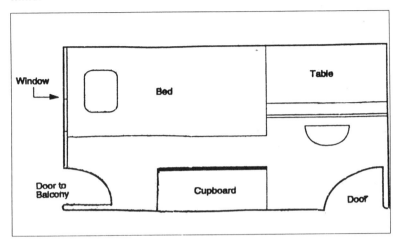

Since your room is rather small, I suggest you move your study-table to where the cupboard is and place the cupboard at the foot of the bed. To cool down your temper, paint your walls apple green.

I would also advise you to make proper use of the bed. When you sleep on the floor, yin *chi* enters your body. An excess of yin *chi* causes arthritis in your old age.

Furthermore, you lose *chi* from your body when your feet faces the door. Thus, no matter how long you sleep, you will always end up lethargic.

Study-table next to door

ENCLOSED IS A plan of my bedroom layout. Is the furniture properly arranged?

Mrs Lilian Pang
Johor Baru

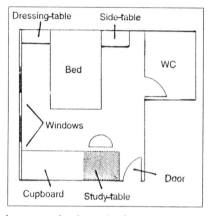

AS YOUR ROOM is quite small, leave your bed where it is; that is the best position for it.

However, you need to reposition your study-table which is next to the door. As the door is considered the threshold of your room, you can be easily distracted by activities outside and may not be able to concentrate on your studies. To enable better concentration, place the table away from the door.

PART
24

Dining Areas and Kitchens

Reserved chair

CAN A VISITOR who often used to sit on the dining-chair belonging to the breadwinner of the family actually take our luck away if he has such intentions?

Is it considered bad feng shui to the family if a deceased relative is buried in water-logged land?

Tradition Seeker
Ipoh

TODAY WE STILL come across concerned, elderly people who warn youngsters not to expose their palms too often to palmist or fortune-tellers. They believe that, lurking among the true practitioners of these arts, would be devious individuals out to siphon off one's luck. How far this is true, is a matter of opinion.

But our elders may be right to a certain extent. When a person visits soothsayers too often, he may become totally confused because of the many different bits of advice he is given.

Again, you should not discount the existence of the black arts which may be precisely what these unscrupulous men use to 'steal' one's good fortune away. If you do fear such things happening, what you can do is to make sure everyone who visits your house knows that the breadwinner's chair is reserved.

As for the second question: a good piece of land should always be chosen as a burial site so that the deceased may rest in peace. This is not just a saying but it is believed that a suitable environment is needed for the deceased to return to the earth (that is, when the body decomposes).

It is indeed bad feng shui for someone to be buried in a water logged area because this condition disrupts the environment and does not allow the body to decompose 'naturally'.

Water and fire

IN MY KITCHEN, THERE is a drain which flows directly underneath the cooker. Its source of water is from the sink and the wash-room.

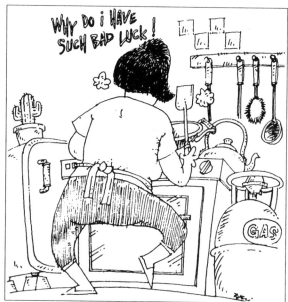

I have had very little luck with 'numbers' and I wonder if this has anything to do with my drainage system.

Mrs S. Siew
Kuala Lumpur

THE STOVE IS a place where family food is prepared. The element that dominates this area is fire. To have water run underneath it is to have problems created because water extinguishes fire. Symbolically, it means thwarting your attempts to eke out a living.

As a remedy, divert the drain to flow in the opposite direction as shown in the diagram.

Exposed to
main entrance

*ENCLOSED IS A sketch plan of my house. How would the feng shui of
the house affect my family and business? How can I rectify any
negative chi?*

Kris Chong
Kuala Lumpur

TO HAVE ONE'S dining area totally exposed towards the main door is
bad feng shui. Food which is served on the table would face the main
door, and would be lost in that direction. As food symbolizes money, it
is said that money is being lost.

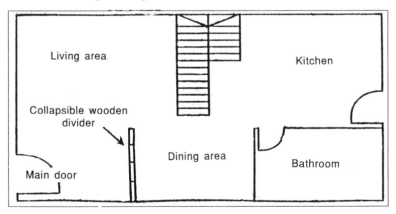

To counter such losses, place a collapsible wooden divider
between the dining area and the main door.

Too close to the living-room

MY MOTHER AND my sister cannot get along well. They quarrel all the time over minor matters, and my mother is very upset over this. She has asked me to consult a geomancer to find out what is wrong with our house and its surroundings. The pre-war house belongs to us but the land belongs to the landlord.

The members of the family are generally healthy, except for some old-age problems.

Kindly suggest some remedy for a more harmonious environment as I would like to see my mother happy.

Anxious Daughter
Penang

YOUR HOUSE SHOWS that formally your kitchen was placed towards the back portion of the house but it was no longer utilized due to the lack of proper drainage. Instead, the kitchen is now placed well towards the front part of the house where it is partitioned next to the living room.

The living-room is a place of rest, and to have the kitchen placed next to it is to invite lots of quarrels among family members because the kitchen symbolizes 'fire'.

The only way to bring harmony back to the house is to move the kitchen back to its original place. The problem then is to find a proper drainage system.

PART
25

Symbols

Eight is enough

*I READ WITH interest your reply to a reader in Petaling Jaya who
asked about the siting of her fish-pond. I also noticed that you
mentioned the ideal number of fish to rear.
I have an aquarium of moderate size in my house. I am rearing
seven fish (three different species) and one lobster—eight in all. Please
advise.*

Tan Bu Ang
Pahang

SINCE YOUR AQUARIUM is inside your house, just stand in the
middle of your room, and, with a compass, determine a suitable place
for it. The best place to put an indoor aquarium is against the north or
east walls.

Your aquarium has seven fish and a lobster, and this should do fine
in terms of harmonic influences. The total number is eight, or *fatt*,
which is auspicious indeed.

Black goldfish

I AM A Form 5 student who will be sitting for my SPM exams soon. My room has three windows that face the west. Recently, a relative who left for the city, gave me a big aquarium. My friends tell me that rearing black goldfish will enhance my feng shui. What say you?

Samson Rugsby
Butterworth

I WOULD LIKE to point out two weaknesses in your room layout as shown in the diagram you gave.

Since your bed and the study-table face the west, it would be very hot in the evenings, so the feng shui here would be negative. Besides, if you were to sit at the table to do some studying, you would find it very warm, and your concentration would be affected.

For a start, you could place the bed away from the window, as shown in the illustration. The study-table can be turned around so that it faces the wall. By leaving the bookshelf where it is, this new

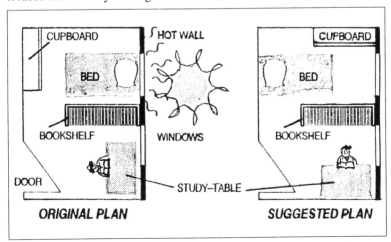

ORIGINAL PLAN   SUGGESTED PLAN

arrangement with your back against the bookshelf while you are studying at the table, symbolizes that you would be backed up by lots of knowledge.

It would be best to leave your aquarium in the hall as your room is already crowded as it is. As for the black goldfish, it is good to rear them if there are a lot of petty thefts and burglaries in the neighbourhood. This will help you from becoming a victim of such vile deeds. Rearing gold goldfish, on the other hand, would enhance one's luck and wealth.

Bird's nest

I AM RENTING a house which faces north. Recently, two small grey and yellow birds built their nest on the ceiling of my porch. Are these newcomers harbingers of misfortune?

Chan Soo Har
Teluk Intan

NORMALLY, A HOUSE facing north is not considered good in terms of feng shui. But when it attracts birds to build their nest within your compound, it certainly tips the balance in your favour.

There is a house in the southern Thai port of Pattani which stands on a dusty street in a row of crumbling buildings. At nesting time, this particular house echoes with the sounds of swiftlets.

These birds, which provide prized bird's nest, bring wealth, to the old woman who lives there. Local lore has it that this house alone is chosen by the birds to nest in because it was once blessed by the townspeople's favourite deity, Lin Ku-Niang.

In your case, one reason the birds would seek out your house in the first place is because they detect 'good vibrations'.

Tortoise

TORTOISE-REARER OF PENANG who wants to know if rearing tortoises in the home prevents good luck and *chi* from entering.

As far as we know, nothing has been said about tortoises preventing good fortune and *chi* from entering the home. To many Chinese, the tortoise is a health-giving food when brewed with a number of herbs.

In ancient times, the tortoise's hard shell would be broken into many pieces and Chinese characters written on them. These pieces would then be used by soothsayers in their divinations.

Tortoises are also reared in many temples—like the Kek Lok Si in Ayer Itam, Penang, and the Sam Poh Tong temple in Ipoh.

Tortoises also have a very long lifespan, some of them spanning to centuries. This sign of longevity is significant for the owner but, because the tortoise is slow, its creeping pace is not in line with the fast-paced lifestyle of today's society. Therefore, not many people like to rear them.

On the other hand, who knows, rearing them in your house or compound may bring you prosperity. Remember the famous fable about the tortoise and the hare—slow and steady wins the race.

Frogs

I AM DEAD broke most of the time. I wonder what has gone wrong with my house's feng shui.

Li
Alor Setar

YOUR HOUSE HAPPENS to end up next to a dead end. Since *chi* is normally taken up by the houses in the front, you will only get what is left over. A telephone cable is also cutting across your pathway

between the gate and the main entrance. This symbolizes a '*potong jalan*' of *chi* in your career.

To create some positive balance place a fountain by the side of your compound to attract *chi*. Stick two small pairs of scissors facing upwards to symbolically snip away the negativeness of the cable. And since your house also faces your neighbour's gate, place a *pakua* to balance the feng shui.

You have placed two stone frogs at the entrance. Normally, frogs attract wealth but since yours are facing an empty field across the road, you get nothing. The best thing to do is remove the frogs.

Dragon and phoenix

I HAVE A picture of a dragon and another picture of a phoenix on the wall of my sitting-room. People have been telling me that these pictures are no good. What do you say?

Follower of Feng Shui
Kuala Lumpur

THE DRAGON AND the phoenix are mystical animals in the Chinese kingdom. These two animals are said to complement one another, so they are always seen together, whether in Chinese New Year cards, paintings or woodcraft.

So it is perfectly alright to hang a picture of these two animals together. Kindly disregard what your friends have been telling you.

Yin and yang

CAN YOU TELL me the correct way to hang a pakua? Which way should the yin and yang symbol (in the middle of the pakua) face?

Cheah Tiat Chuan
Johor Baru

THE CORRECT MANNER of placing this symbol is as shown in the diagram below.

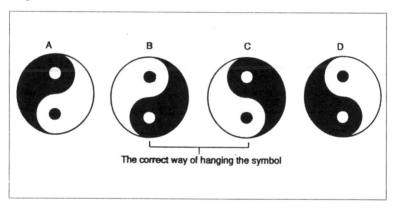

The correct way of hanging the symbol

Clock

WHEN A CLOCK faces a staircase, is it true that this can ward off evil forces that descend from it?

Believer
Prai

IN FENG SHUI, ordinary wall clocks would not stop bad *chi* from coming in, but a grandfather clock with a moving pendulums is believed to be able to deflect or ward off *sha chi* and evil forces.

Ceiling beams

WHAT HAPPENS WHEN there are several beams criss-crossing, each other in the living-room? If there is a problem, please advise how to rectify it.

May Cheong
Selangor

BEAMS VISIBLE NEAR the ceiling would create an unbalance in *chi* in the room. Rectify the situation by situation placing a firecracker in the right position. The firecracker symbolizes a dynamite, so placing one on the centre of a beam would connote 'blowing up' the beam. This is applicable if the beam is in a horizontal position.

However, in your living-room where there is criss-cross of ceiling beams, placing firecrackers on them would make the room look inelegant. The best way to restore the balance of *chi* in your living-room is to build a suspended ceiling.